PENNY-PINCHERS

Financial Self-Management – A Practical Guide

A Pocket Book of Money-Saving Tips, Tricks and Tools

Adam James

This publication is designed to provide competent and reliable information regarding the subject matter covered. However, it is sold with the understanding that the author and publisher are not engaged in rendering legal, financial, or other professional advice. Laws and practices vary from country to country and if legal or other expert assistance is required, the services of a professional should be sought. In short, the author and publisher disclaim any liability that is incurred from the use or application of the contents of this book.

For Laura Allen

This work, though modest in scope, would have remained forever in obscurity without your love and support.

And a special thanks to my mother, who, in her own special way, inculcated in me a saver's mindset and instilled money management discipline.

Contents

Introduction	1
Financial Strategy	18
The Rules	**49**
Rule 1: Spend Half, Save Half (aka the 50/50 Maxim)	50
Rule 2: Structure Your Accounts	52
Rule 3: Ask Yourself These Three Important Questions	56
Rule 4: Delay Gratification	57
Rule 5: Create a Budget	64
Rule 6: Cut the Credit Cards	69
Rule 7: Pay Yourself First	82
Rule 8: Form Good Financial Habits and Break the Bad Ones	89
Rule 9: Regularly Review Your Finances	96
Rule 10: Live Within Your Means	105
Examples of Financial Idiocy: An Interlude	**112**
Tips, Tricks and Tools	**127**
Tip 1: Monitoring Expenditure	129
Tip 2: Have a Secret Stash	134
Tip 3: Curb Runaway Spending	137
Tip 4: The Law of Incremental Accumulation (LIA)	141

Tip 5: Sign Over Power of Attorney   146
Tip 6: 30-Day Spending Fast   149
Tip 7: Make it *VISIBLE!*   155
Tip 8: Treasure Trove   162
Tip 9: The Death Pledge (aka the Mortgage)   190
Tip 10: Advance Your Knowledge   212

References   **230**

Index   **226**

Introduction

So what's it all about?

In a nutshell *Penny-Pinchers* is a compendium of non-pretentious common-sense methods of saving money on essentials – such as bills and their ilk – enabling you to have more to pop in the piggy bank or spend on the things you want. But the buck doesn't stop there. The scope of this informative endeavour encompasses many methodologies of money management including, most importantly, showing you how to avoid debilitating debt. In addition, and this is one of the primary pillars upholding the *Penny-Pinchers'* pantheon, you will receive a crash course in financial strategy, the purpose of which is to enable you to eradicate debt while pursuing financial security.

At a time when UK household debt has exceeded £450 billion – nearly half a trillion, if you can believe it – a project such as this, modest in scale though it is, has never been more needed. At the time of writing, the average home is chained to a £15,000 ball of debt, and spending trends suggest that that ball is steadily increasing in size. Much of this debt is unsupported – i.e. it is not backed against a capital asset such as property. Unsupported debt is arguably the most pernicious kind because it was most likely amassed through gratuitous consumerism and/or undisciplined spending habits, which is most likely owed to credit cards, banks and other usurious lenders.

If those indebted households took a page out of the *Penny-Pinchers* book and adopted the principles herein inscribed, that

£450 billion would decrease precipitously, much to the annoyance of unscrupulous lenders.

The primary aim of *Penny-Pinchers* is to help you find financial security.

Its other aims are:

- To help you save money on necessities (bills and so on) so that you have more to spend and enjoy on non-necessities.
- To offer advice on debt avoidance, including equipping you with the tools to break the fetters of debilitating debt.
- To help you cultivate monetary discipline.
- To offer methods to improve your accounting.
- To arm you with the necessary weapons to fight off pernicious fiscal expenditure.
- To help you develop strategies that will move you from the financial slough to fields of gold.

The *Penny-Pinchers* pledge

- To provide you with valuable advice that, if implemented, can and will make a genuine difference in your life.
- To disseminate a wealth of quality knowledge and information that is tried and tested and thus proven to yield positive results.
- To suggest clear and simple methods of ameliorating your financial status so that you can start to enjoy money.

What to expect

Throughout this book you will discover many simple, easy-to-use, tried-and-tested ideas that will enable you to save money, carefully manage your accounts, avoid debt and, if you're in debt, show you how to get out of it. Perhaps a point of clarification is required before we proceed any further. Please do not read in the use of words like 'simple' or 'easy' any demerit or deprecation of the information contained within this book. That would be a mistake. I'm of the opinion that the best advice, the advice most eminently actionable, is inherently uncomplicated. Take, for example, the sagacious utterances of the great twentieth-century economist extraordinaire, John Maynard Keynes:

> Provided it is agreed that income is equal to the value of current output, that current investment is equal to that part of current input which is not consumed, and that saving is equal to the excess of income over consumption ... the equality of saving and investment necessarily follow.
>
> [...]
>
> Hence, in the aggregate the excess of income over consumption, which we call saving, cannot differ from the addition to capital equipment which we call investment. And similarly with net saving and investment. Saving, in fact, is a mere residual. The decisions to consume and the decisions to invest between them determine incomes. Assuming that the decisions to invest become effective, they must in doing so either curtail consumption or expand income.
>
> [...]
>
> Clearness of mind on this matter is best reached, perhaps, by thinking in terms of decisions to consume (or refrain from consuming) rather than decisions to save. A decision to consume

or not to consume truly lies within the power of the individual; so does the decision to invest or not to invest.[1]

So what did we take from that then? Well, unless you have a degree from the London School of Economics, probably not much. But if we were to heap those many confusing syllables into a pan and pop it on high heat for ten minutes or so we might be able to boil away the superfluous leaving the essence. It could perhaps be summarised thus:

If we're clever and don't spend more than we earn, we'll have a bit left over to either save or invest. And if we want to increase our savings and/or investments, we must either (a) reduce consumption or (b) increase our income. Ideally we should do both.

Perhaps I'm not exactly on the money with my layman's attempt at deciphering Keynes' highly intellectualised theorising. However, I'm quite confident that the majority of readers will understand my condensed encapsulation. Indeed, not only will they understand it better, but they will immediately identify a causal relationship between income, spending, and savings and investments, and understand how they impact each other. And that is the pre-eminent quality of all proceeding advice: it is both accessible and actionable. For what good is advice in such important matters as personal finance if it requires specialist subject knowledge to understand it or professional training to make use of it? When someone is drowning, they require

---

[1] John Maynard Keynes, *The Essential Keynes* (Penguin Classic, 2015), pp. 191 and 192.

immediate assistance, such as a buoyancy aid, a friendly dolphin or a strong swimmer. What they don't need is a flat-pack self-assembly dinghy that requires five frustrating hours to make seaworthy.

For those who are struggling to swim in the turbulent and often dangerous seas of personal finance, this book is intended to be that much-needed friendly dolphin on whose back you can hitch a ride to dry land.

What not to expect

This book does not provide financial advice regarding stocks and shares or any form of 'investment vehicle'. Although it is true that a couple of people have done really rather well out of the old stock market trading/investment racket, millions haven't; many have lost a lot, and some have lost everything. Here's a bit of anecdotal spit and polish to add some shine to that statement.

At a dinner party a while back I struck up a conversation with the host's wife. It transpired that we had quite a bit in common: we both played the guitar (she played classical, I play electric); we both enjoyed exercising more than we should; we both enjoyed strong black coffee and musing over matters philosophical; and we both were amateur enthusiasts of that quasi-science known as economics. The moment we were on mutual intellectual ground I began gabbing about the strikingly accurate Pareto 80/20 law and the immense intelligence of John Maynard Keynes. Meanwhile, she extolled the brilliance of contemporary investors – Warren Buffett, Ray Dalio, Paul Tudor Jones, to name the most prominent.

I asked her, as this seemed to be where her interest in economics lay, if she herself had ever gambled on the stock exchange. She said she had, although she didn't much appreciate my making a comparison to so low and base an addiction ('The stock market is not a casino!' she snapped). I didn't expect this and, taken aback as I was, swivelled on my chair to face her fully. I waited patiently for her to provide a summary of the financial forecast of the S&P 500. But all of a sudden she became uncharacteristically reticent. Doing away with decorum and propriety I probed her on her investment portfolio. 'How's it doing – up or down?' I asked.

Reluctantly she told me that she had 'blundered' not only with her first 'picks' but also her timing. The companies she had chosen were now buried in the rubble of the 2008 financial crash, along with the £60,000 she had invested in them.

Writing about this now I can readily recall being overcome by hot sweats at the mere thought of seeing such a substantial sum of money slipping into the abyss without leaving so much as a trace. What amazed me most was that, ten years later, she was at the slots again!

When she told me this, my eyebrows floated off my face for a second time. On seeing the surprise on my face she explained that this roll of the die was different because she'd learned from her previous mistakes.

I asked her what she'd learned.

For starters, she said, she had diversified her portfolio, the equivalent of not putting all your eggs in one basket – in investment parlance this is called 'reducing your exposure'. I was amazed that she hadn't done that at the beginning. That's one of the ten commandments of investing: *thou shalt diversify*! Also, she strictly prohibited herself from checking stock fluctuations every five minutes and reduced her checks to once a day. (She told me that when she first started investing she'd become so addicted to checking her share prices that she began doing it at work, which eventually resulted in her dismissal!) And finally, the last lesson she had learned was not to offload stock when share prices dipped, under any circumstances. The amateur investor buys high and sells low, as the saying goes.

While listening to her I felt a sense of admiration at her courageous get-up-dust-yourself-off-and-try-again attitude. Most people I'm sure would have walked away from the table after seeing their entire life savings disappear in the blink of an eye (those with a soft constitution may have even sought succour at the end of a rope). It was then, as I was mulling this over, that I unwittingly made a grave transgression in investor etiquette: I asked her to divulge her current portfolio, which is the equivalent of asking a poker player if you can see their hand. She shrank back in horror. 'An investor never discloses the contents of their portfolio!' she said.

But I've never been one for convention, so I pressed her again. 'What, do you think I'm going to steal your investment strategy?' I said, affecting a haughty demeanour. 'I've neither the inclination nor the psychological and emotional durability necessary to spin the stock market roulette wheel. The content of your portfolio is safe with me.'

She obviously took this as a compliment and proceeded to give me the grand tour on her iPad of the eight companies she had 'bought'. Instantly I thought she'd made yet another blunder: to me eight didn't seem quite diverse enough. I'm sure I'd read in *The Economist* that a diversified portfolio should be comprised of no fewer than sixteen companies. I kept this information to myself. As she flicked through her electronic portfolio I noticed a stock graph that showed a precipitous decline, over which a thick red X had been scored, much like the paint daubed on the doors of people infected with the bubonic plague. Pointing, I asked her what had gone on there. With a deep sigh she explained that the company – an Icelandic bank (I almost burst out laughing) – had, for reasons she didn't know nor seem to understand, 'bottomed out' (meaning the stock had plummeted).

The £4,000 worth of stock she had invested in that Icelandic bank wouldn't have covered the price of a flat white at Starbucks had she cashed it in. Pulling the optimistic wool over her own eyes she claimed that it wasn't bothering her in the least, it being a natural and normal occurrence in the stock market, and that while before she would have sold, now she would leave her investment as she was sure it would pick back up again.

I wasn't convinced by either her optimism or her forecasting.

Later on, when I returned home, I reflected on our conversation. Coincidental as it was, before speaking with her I had been seriously toying with the idea of developing a portfolio of my own. I instantly hit the delete button on that idea. Also, I couldn't help but notice the emotional turmoil she seemed to be suffering. This I am certain was a consequence of the constant anxiety induced by worrying over share-price fluctuations. Why put yourself through that? I remember thinking. For the meagre returns she stood to make on the £32,000 she had invested, all that worry and stress just didn't seem worth it. Even if all of her stock did well (and a sizeable chunk of it wasn't) earning an annual return of 6% her investment would only increase it by about £2,000 a year. Yes, I concede that's a significantly greater return than you'd ever get from a savings account. However, your money is many orders of magnitude safer in a savings account. Perhaps a better investment strategy would be found in property; bricks and mortar are much securer investments (though less of the 'much' after 2008!).

Since that chance encounter I've dispelled the fantasy of becoming a billionaire investor. But just because I'm a spineless coward doesn't mean *you* have to be. The above account of one investor's disastrous experience is not an attempt to discourage those who are flirting with the idea of gambling on the stock market (if you want other dire accounts, read Sir Walter Scott's journal, or join a forum for traders and investors). I included it only to illustrate the inhospitable and unforgiving financial environment that is the stock market and as a means of substantiating my supposition that only a reckless lunatic would enter that environment without first seeking serious training from an experienced professional. I am neither.

Consequently, if you feel compelled, as Ray Dalio coined it, to play 'poker with the best poker players on earth', and you have a burning desire to 'master the game' (in the words of Tony Robbins), this book is not for you.[2] Consider instead Van K. Tharp's *Trade Your Way to Financial Freedom* and William O'Neil's *How to Make Money in Stocks*, both brilliant beginner's guides to trading.

Penny-Pinchers, by contrast, aims to propagate safe practical advice; advice that, if acted upon, will not result in the demolition of your piggy bank. It's about pursuing financial security, avoiding debt and discovering ways of saving money on those things in life we have to buy but don't want to so that we have more to spend on things we do want to buy. But most of all it's a book about developing monetary discipline.

---

[2] Ray Dalio quoted in Tony Robbins, *Money: Master the Game* (Simon & Schuster, 2016), p. 21.

Why, out of the plethora of financial books available, should I choose this one?

I'm not so blinded by self-conceit to believe that the information contained in this book is in any way original, paradigm-shifting or revolutionary. Much of what follows can be found, I have no doubt, in the store cupboard of common sense. (You hardly need to have squandered a quarter of a million on a degree from Harvard Business School to understand the detrimental impact of spending more than you earn.) The rest has been gleaned from age-old financial wisdom, which anyone can pick up if they're willing to listen, from personal experience (also known as making mistakes and learning from them) and from the infosphere colloquially called the World Wide Web. Actually, I would confidently wager a week's wage that there is not a single syllable among the two hundred-odd thousand contained here that could not be pilfered free of charge from the internet – that's if you have the time and inclination to sift through the shit-ton of chaff to find that one strand of wheat.

My honesty negates any possibility of a career in politics or public relations. But that, as I see it, is where the strength of this book and its author's approach lie – to wit telling it as it is and not beating around the bush in the telling.

It has not escaped my notice that the ethos espoused in most popular self-help/self-development books is one of epicurean ease and excess. If you were to believe the teachings of the more successful leaders in this genre, and there are many, all you have to do to get immense wealth, immense health and a perfect figure is flip open a laptop, molest a mouse and crack out a couple of dumb-bell curls. Few of these self-styled gurus endeavour to make it explicitly clear to their readership from the outset that help and development will never come – will never be yours – unless you're prepared to put in the effort, apply the techniques and exercise that imperative yet often atrophied muscle called self-discipline. And even then you still might not achieve your ambition. It's obvious why they do this – for truth seldom sells.

So I say to you – because I care not a damn about sales and ill-gotten social kudos, only about creating value – if you're not prepared to toil, to impose lifestyle restrictions and to cultivate cast-iron self-discipline, DO NOT read this book for it will be useless to you. Instead of parting with the pocket change that it costs, go take a punt on a lottery ticket or treat yourself to a cup of sweetened full-fat milk from one of those overpriced coffee houses. I only want readers who are serious and willing to graft. If you're not, I ask that you quit reading and peaceably pass on by. But if, on the other hand, you are serious about financial self-management and are prepared to make some sacrifices, I can confidently predict that you will profit from the teachings and advice soon to follow.

That, I think, brings us nicely back to the opening question: why should I choose this book over the competition? Read on and your question will be answered.

How it came to be

Before we get into the more interesting *proactive* stuff, let me take up a couple of minutes of your time to explain why I wrote this book. I recognise that it might come across as a touch egocentric and self-indulgent for an author to expect the reader to give a single toss about how or why their book was conceived. However, I believe that a bit of background insight will elucidate the altruistic intention of this endeavour. You should know that whatever financial predicament has brought you to my door I can in some way relate to – not only relate to but understand. It is through this understanding that, though I do not know you, I can sympathise with your situation. I am reaching out with what I hope is a helping hand.

I follow some simple rules and monetary methodologies which keep me on the financial straight and narrow. I believe they can do the same for you too. These rules and methods would no doubt be laughed out of any respectable financial advisory office, and if they were mentioned in the presence of an accountant I might expect to be mocked or assaulted with an abacus. Yet for the average person – who merely wants to avoid debt, pay their bills on time, build up a savings account and have a bit left over for the things that make life more pleasurable – the teachings in this book will assist them on the journey to their financial ideal.

I developed these rules and methodologies when I myself slipped into a chasm of debt. Breathe a sigh of relief – this is not that bit where I regale you with a tale of woe about how I lost everything and managed, through sheer grit and determination, to claw my way back to solvency. However, I did fall deeper and deeper into a financial funk from which I was unable to extricate myself for many years. In a nutshell this is what happened. I began spending more each month than I earned. After a time I found myself lost in a dark wood of debt. Somehow I managed to rack up thousands on credit cards and I habitually lived in my overdraft. This was one of the most unpleasant times of my life.

When I reflect on my past behaviour I am appalled by my ignorance and inability to exercise the necessary discipline that would have prevented all that misery. But had I not made those mistakes, I would never have learned how to fix them. And I wouldn't have written this book and we wouldn't be enjoying this pleasant conversation.

Now, I don't want to mislead the reader into thinking that I was a complete financial train wreck. In the grand scheme of things the debt I'd accrued and the laissez-faire attitude I'd cultivated toward personal finances was positively angelic when compared to some satanic spenders. A paltry three grand in the red is nothing. I've known people who were ten, twenty, even a hundred thousand pounds in debt. For someone who has dug themselves into such a deep hole, a few thousand quid equates to little more than another shovelful. But for me, three thousand was far too much. I'm one of those people who cannot be bought anything without instantly being assailed by the compulsion to reciprocate. And if, on one of those rare blue-moon occasions where I've had to borrow a couple of pennies because I was caught short, I would ensure that that money was returned in full the next day, usually with interest.

So what had happened, then, to this penny-pinching miser? How did I manage to land myself in such a sizeable sum of debt? Well, it's quite simple really. I began living beyond my means. I was struggling to delay gratification (an endemic problem of this materialistic age). If I wanted something, I would purchase it, regardless of whether I had the coin or not. And I was in a state of complete denial, probably the worst, most sinful thing of all. I refused to acknowledge this problem, which was spiralling out of control.

What does it look like when someone loses control of their finances? They bin bank statements before opening them. They draw money from an account that's already overdrawn. They borrow money from their nearest and dearest just to stay afloat until payday. They visit Cash Converters to sell off personal effects at obscenely discounted rates. These are just some of the hallmarks of the person on the road to financial ruin.

If you see shades of yourself in any of these examples, then immediate action is required!

> Mr Micawber was right on the money when he said: 'Annual income twenty pounds, annual expenditure nineteen six, result happiness. Annual income twenty pounds, annual expenditure twenty pounds ought and six, result misery' (Charles Dickens, *David Copperfield*).

During a brief moment of sobriety after years of intoxication I decided to do something about my sorry state of affairs. At the end of an hour-long stern self-talking too, swiftly followed by a sharp kick up the arse, I took action. Because my pay cheque covered my overdraft, leaving only £10 to spare, for one month I confined myself to what I renamed the Hermitage (aka my home). No going out, no socialising, no coffee shops, no internet spending, no fiscal transactions whatsoever! For four agonisingly long weeks I lived like a monk in a cloistered cell. Extreme situations call for extreme measures. It was one of the longest months of my life, but it did the trick (I've now developed this into a personal disciplinary exercise that I call 'financial fasting' whereby for a given period of time (usually a month) once or twice a year, I do not spend a single dime. For more on financial fasting see **Tip 6 of Tips, Tricks and Tools**).

After some two years of drowning ever deeper in debt, I managed to get myself back in the boat out of which I had fallen. And by god did I feel good when my account was in credit! Each payday was like winning the lottery. The relief of finally being financially stable enough to start paying off those credit cards was in itself a momentous achievement. But when I finally paid off that credit card debt, when I finally severed those shackles – well, that moment was indescribable. I want that for you!

Once safely aboard, I fashioned a set of rules that I decided I would use to navigate the course of my finances for the rest of my life. I also devised some simple tools and tricks that enabled me to save money on the things I really don't like parting with cash for but have to (household bills, for example), leaving me with more money for things that I want – such as guitars, books, holidays and meals out.

But before we venture into the rules, tools and tricks, we're going to spend some time considering the concept of financial strategy, the consequences of failing to adequately implement a strategy and exploring how to apply that strategy once we have created one. In addition, I will walk you through the world of austerity and show you the financial force that this much-despised concept can exert.

Come on then, let's get going.

Financial Strategy

First things first. Before we delve into the vault and attempt to pack our pockets with money-saving ideas we must first learn how to pick the lock. Above all else, it is of primary importance if you are drowning in debt or your head is bobbing on the surface of your overdraft to develop a financial amelioration strategy.

The difference between a goal and a strategy

Let's begin by outlining precisely what constitutes a strategy and why it should not be mistaken for a goal (objective or vision). The simplest distinction between a strategy and a goal is that a strategy is active and a goal is passive. A goal is a destination that exists in a stationary state somewhere out there. If we want to arrive at that destination, then we must devise a means of getting there. This is where strategy steps onto the stage. Strategy is all those components required to help you reach your destination; it's the mode of transportation, the fuel to power the vehicle, the map (or satnav) and any provisions you might need en route.

Of course, there are good ways to reach a destination and there are bad ways. In his book *Good Strategy/Bad Strategy*, Richard Rumelt tells us that good strategy is 'primarily about deciding what is truly important and focusing resources and action on that object'.[1] So, in the pursuit of arriving at that destination there are a number of options available to the would-be traveller. He could (a) just wing it – hop into his car, pull off the drive in a random direction and hope for the best. Alternatively, he could (b) from

---

[1] Richard Rumelt, *Good Strategy/Bad Strategy* (Profile Books, 2017), p. 90.

the comfort of his armchair, plan a route using a map, or punch an address into the satnav (or both, the map serving as a backup should technology let him down). In addition to planning a route, he could also prepare an inventory of provisions, food and water for the journey and perhaps a variety of music to mitigate the boredom of watching the rolling road. (A couple of summers back I travelled through Europe by car and foolishly took only two CDs – an eclectic assortment of Moby tracks and a chill-out dance mix. Suffice to say, after nearly fifty hours of driving over the course of a week, I now hate Moby and chill-out dance music.) If he were really savvy, he might also plot out appropriate places to pull over for a comfort break along the route. This is starting to develop into a sound strategy.

Now, if I were to ask you which of the two strategic examples – (a) wing it, or (b) plan ahead – stood the best chance of aiding our hypothetical traveller to successfully arrive at his desired destination, which would you put your money on: a or b? It's a no-brainer! But here's the thing, if the traveller presented you with the goal of reaching destination X, in the absence of any strategy it would seem plausible, even if they planned to wing it. This is why a goal should never be pursued in the absence of a strategy for even the simplest goal will be prohibitively unachievable if approached haphazardly.

In fact we could go further and say that a goal is entirely worthless without some sort of strategy. At the risk of wearing out my metaphor, imagine if someone said to you that they had set themselves the goal of arriving at destination X before lunch yet you knew they did not possess the means or equipment to achieve that goal. What would you think? What would you say to

19

them? Well, you'd certainly be forgiven for thinking them a little simple and, exercising a spot of diplomacy, you'd probably advise them to reconsider their goal.

To sum up then, strategy is not a goal (objective or vision) but the pre-planned process by which you intend to achieve that goal. As Rumelt says, at its essence 'a good strategy has coherence, coordinating actions, policies, and resource [allocation] so as to accomplish an important end'.[2] The strategy is the road map and resources required to help you to arrive at your desired destination. However, I should conclude this short exposition on strategy with a caveat. Though it is true that strategy is a means of navigation and transportation, like a vehicle without fuel and a driver, it will never get you to your destination if you lack the motivation and discipline to take decisive and sustained action.

To exemplify this point I will now turn to two contrasting case studies, which will demonstrate the outcome of (a) failing to implement strategy, and (b) following the strategy.

Case study 1
Having become thoroughly fed up with paid employment, with working for misanthropic managers in toxic organisations, Steve decided to put his knowledge, skills and experience to use and embarked on a small business venture (a health and well-being service). His goal was firstly to generate an additional income with the view of developing it into his primary mode of employment at a later stage.

---

[2] Rumelt, *Good Strategy/Bad Strategy*, p. 11.

Now Steve's goal was, by today's standards, relatively simple and achievable. He possessed the skills, knowledge and experience, and he had access to abundant resources to reach the appropriate clientele. Really, all he had to do was pop online, create a website, market his services and, with his hook baited and plonked in the fecund social media waters, wait until a few fish swam by and took a bite. That was the crux of Steve's strategic plan. But alas, he likes to whittle his time away in the company of Greek philosophers or imitating seventies rock icons on his knock-off beaten-up Fender Stratocaster (his icons of choice include Clapton, Hendrix and Page).

A year on, Steve's website resembled one of those partially complete timeshares you see littering the Costa del Sol. As a consequence of conflating priorities with pastimes, his strategic plan wasn't adequately implemented. The result? No fish nibbling at his hook – because his hook, along with the bait, was still in his fishing tackle box.

Case study 2
Having become thoroughly fed up with paid employment, with working for misanthropic managers in toxic organisations, Laura decided to put to use her extensive knowledge, skills and experience and embarked on a small business venture (a coaching and counselling service). Her goals were a mirror image of Steve's, viz. to generate a secondary income with the view of developing it into her primary mode of employment. Being the undiagnosed entrepreneur that she was Laura decided to use a strategic plan that was the spit of Steve's – after all, why reinvent the wheel?

On blowing off the dust she made a few minor alterations to the means by which the plan would reach its target audience and set about implementing the strategy. In less than a week she'd designed and published a respectable website. Using this as her primary platform she embarked on an aggressive marketing campaign, nailing business cards, leaflets and flyers into every inanimate object within a five-square-mile radius and launched a series of social media advertisements. Within three months Laura had netted her first client; within six months that one had climbed to four. And within a year she had ten people on a waiting list.

Comparing and contrasting the two case studies we can clearly see the mistake the fool featured in the first example made. Up to the point of implementing the strategy, Steve's and Laura's goals, and the process by which their goals were to be reached, were identical. But the outcomes were worlds apart. Because Steve procrastinated in the execution of his strategy, he failed to reach his destination. In fact, he didn't succeed in getting to the end of his driveway. Meanwhile Laura was well on her way, and enjoying the journey to boot.

It is from these case studies that we take the most important lesson: strategy is about *action*, about *doing* something.

Now that we fully understand what a strategy is and why it is important to implement one, we can turn our attention to developing financial strategies that will:

- break an overdraft cycle;
- prevent and reverse the perpetuation of debt;

- improve financial health;
- increase savings; and
- usher in much-needed monetary discipline.

How to develop a financial strategy

At the heart of any strategy lies its kernel. The kernel is your purpose, your motivation. Thus, in order for it to be effective, your strategy must be shaped around a coherent kernel. So before spending time strategising, you must first uncover, then define as simply and accurately as possible, exactly what your kernel is.

Say you've amassed credit card debt to the tune of £6,000. It's only now that you decide it's imperative to take action lest you slip into the abyss of financial ruin. When you sit down to review your finances you quickly realise that the problems are many and varied and that the £6,000 debt you've been ignoring for the past twelve months is just one of many ugly heads that you need to sever and cauterise. The trouble with a situation such as this is separating the clutter from the kernel – what to ignore and what to focus on. Most people, I believe, would fixate on that £6,000 debt. However, as I see it, that would be a mistake. 'But surely such a sizeable sum of debt must be placed at the head of your list of financial priorities?' No, not necessarily. Here's why.

Let's assume that as well as carrying around six thousand bricks on your back you're also living hand to mouth; that is, your pay only just covers your overdraft and in a couple of days you'll be financing daily life with borrowed money. That is an unpleasant place to be, and if you are in a position like that, with next to no

23

money for the month, you would be wise to make that the kernel around which you tailor your financial strategy.

Why?

Because how are you ever going to reduce that debt if you haven't money enough to procure the bare necessities?

Okay, for this exercise I'm going to imagine that I've convinced you that the pursuit of financial stability takes precedence over servicing debt. Now that you've established and defined your motivation, your task is to develop a strategy that, when implemented, will enable you to reach your destination. Below I have created such a strategy. But remember, it is a hypothetical example designed merely to demonstrate the characteristics and principles of strategy building. From it you should draw only the information and inspiration needed to create your own.

To kick things off, I've created a fictitious incomings/outgoings chart. This chart will act as the body around which you can tailor your strategy. The goal of your strategy, remember, is to obtain financial stability so that you can start servicing that debt.

Incomings/outgoings

	Incoming	Outgoing
Monthly income (after tax)	£1,500	
Mortgage		£400
Utilities (combined)		£150
Car insurance		£30
Car running costs		£50

Home/contents insurance		£20
Monthly groceries (estimated)		£150
Netflix subscription		£10
Mobile phone contract		£50
Living expenses		£100
Miscellaneous		£100
Overdraft repayment		£400
Outgoings total		**£1,460**
Cash remaining each month	£40	

After spending twenty agonising minutes revising your finances, the above chart is the mouldy fruit of your labour. Though it is true that such a litany of financial mismanagement is certainly nothing to be proud of, you should be proud that you've taken this most important of steps and feel somewhat relieved that your financial inadequacies are now out in the open. But before we move on to develop a strategy, I've got a task for you to complete. Don't worry, it's not too taxing. What I would like you to do is go get a pen, preferably a highlighter, and in the chart above put a bright line through those outgoings that you believe need attention. Once you've highlighted them, number them in order of priority, 1 being the outgoing that needs most attention. Go do that now. I'll wait for you.

Done it? I'm guessing that you've probably highlighted outgoings such as Netflix and Miscellaneous, while awarding the honour of highest priority to the overdraft repayment. If you have done this, or something close to it, then you were partly right. But by highlighting and scoring the overdraft, you have taken a wrong turn. Any guesses as to why? That's correct: the overdraft, unlike all the other outgoings, is not in your power to control. If you're

£400 in the red, then that's what you owe the bank, and they'll have their pound of flesh even if they have to cut you down to the financial bone (the bastards!). However, if you're frittering away fifty squid on a mobile phone contract or spunking a hundred smackeroonies up the wall on living expenses, these outgoings are well within your power to change. It is through this process that we will bring about the change that is to form the foundation of our strategy.

> As the Greek stoic and freed slave Epictetus advised, we ought to 'Make the best use of what is in our power, and treat the rest in accordance with nature.'

Here's how to proceed. Taking the most outrageous colour highlighter you can find, such as one of those radioactive bingo blotters, expose all 'non-essential' outgoings; that is, outgoings that if you reduce or stop them you won't receive threatening letters or court orders or return home after a hard day at the office to find a pair of bald-headed debt collectors standing menacingly on your doorstep. Once you have highlighted all those non-essential outgoings, place them in a box labelled exactly that – non-essentials. Now do the same with essentials. If you bothered to play my strategic game you should have produced something that looks like this:

Non-essentials		Essentials	
Netflix subscription	£10	Mortgage	£400
Mobile phone contract	£50	Utilities (combined)	£150
Miscellaneous	£100	Car insurance	£30

Living expenses[3]	£100	Car running costs	£50
		Home/contents insurance	£20
		Monthly groceries	£150

I'm going to assume that you're a good student and diligently completed the task. So now that you have created two boxes your next task is to strategise ways which you can either reduce or, better still, remove the non-essential outgoings. I know for some this is going to be quite painful. But if you truly wish to improve your financial situation sacrifices must be made (this should come as no surprise; I did warn the reader in the introduction). You need to cull as many of those non-essentials as possible. Personally, I would cancel the Netflix subscription. That way you can, with little to no effort, immediately start reducing your monthly outgoings. With just a few strokes of the computer keyboard you could save yourself £120 a year. That's a positive step forward.

Next you could consider trimming down that mobile phone contract. Or, if you're like me and your social life resembles that of a Benedictine monk, completely cut yourself free from that ball and chain and enjoy the pleasant feeling of once again being able to walk without fetters. By god you'll feel better for it! No

---

[3] It might seem odd placing 'living' expenses in the non-essentials category – 'Is not *living* an essential?' you might well ask, trying but failing to suppress those sarcastic undertones. Of course, yes, it is essential to live; however, I see living expenses as luxuries: meals out, treats, an Americano and almond croissant on the way to work, an end-of-the-week celebratory bevvy with your bestie, etc., etc.

longer will you be a slave to (I'm guessing) the Apple corporation. By moving to a cheaper service provider or cancelling your contract completely you stand to save between £30 and £50 every month. Right there, with so simple a reorganisation of your outgoings, you could be better off by up to £600 a year!

I'll stop there. By now I'm quite certain that you understand the process and can continue to apply it without further tutelage. The strategic steps you have taken thus far on your way to financial stability have been to identify those outgoings that you can reduce or stop immediately. But of course, exposing non-essential outgoings on paper is not enough. 'Strategy,' remember, 'is about action, about doing something.'

Once they are identified you should sever the fetters as soon as possible. I recommend doing that right this second – no time like the present! Every time a saving is made by employing this strategic technique, the money must be directed to servicing that £400 overdraft. But you shouldn't stop there. You should sally forth on these new-found wings of motivation to see if savings can be made with your *essential* outgoings. For they can often be reduced too.

As I write I am transitioning between mortgage providers – never a pleasant experience and one that requires you, the paying customer, to leap through myriad burning bureaucratic hoops. My current deal, coupled with the current interest rate, sees me paying a monthly mortgage bill of £1,058! And it is truly horrible to see that sum sucked out of your account almost the second it's deposited. During an idle moment at my desk I once worked out that the first two weeks at work each month were spent earning to pay a loan that was conjured out of thin air. And across the five years I've been paying my mortgage, more than 80% has serviced the interest (an arbitrary figure set by some pen-pushing dweeb from the Bank of England).

So, when my fixed-term came to an end, I diligently hunted down a different lender who could offer me a lower interest rate. Thanks to the internet this is not the laborious, time-consuming rigmarole it used to be. In under an hour of searching I located a lender offering a much lower interest rate. Over the same term – 25 years – not only did my monthly repayments drop to £763 – a saving of nearly £300 a month (£3,600 over the year) – but I would also save some £36,000 in interest repayments. If I hadn't bothered to change mortgage provider and seek out a better deal, if I had stayed on the old rate for another five years, I would have paid an additional £17,000!

What am I saying here? This: it pays to spend a bit of time scratching around for a better deal, and you should do this for every essential outgoing. Every pound you save can be directed to more pernicious debt – overdrafts, credit cards and their cruel counterparts – and then eventually, when you are on the financial straight and narrow, to savings and the things you want.

Remember: if ever you find yourself in a sticky financial situation, your first and last priority is to focus on those things that are within your immediate power of control.

Austerity

What is austerity? Well, that's what the government does when it's bankrupt, both financially and creatively. The word connotes a Scrooge-like existence where a poor, niggardly creature refuses to turn on the heating in the dead of winter so as to save a couple of shillings, settling instead for a moth-eaten tartan blanket. The diet of this miserable miser would make prison food seem like fine dining and his home would be as barren as the ascetic's cloistered cell.

Austerity, then, is the state of imposing severe and strict limitations on the quantity of a resource consumed. Austerity measures could be imposed on energy, food and commodity consumption. In short, austerity can, like an arrow, be aimed at a specific target, or, like an enveloping blanket, be flung wide open. In this next section of our strategy to achieving financial stability we will consider a number of ways that we can tighten our purse strings without degenerating into a mouldy old miser.

So what does it mean to impose austerity measures? It's quite simple really. To enforce a period of austerity requires that we reduce or cease spending and slow or cut consumption. For a pre-specified period of time (1, 6 or 12 months) we would live well within our means and stop all unnecessary or superfluous purchases. Here's an example. If, like me, you enjoy whiling away your Sunday mornings in a coffee shop, drinking the obvious and eating croissants, you might decide to stop these visits – not permanently but perhaps for a month or two, or until you've extricated yourself from the financial funk you're in. Alternatively, you might cut the frequency of visits down to once or twice a month.

By tightening your belt and retrenching you'll be surprised at how much money you can save. Of course, the effectiveness of austerity is compounded when it is enacted wholesale – that is, across all aspects of your spending practices. We wouldn't *just* reduce the amount of coffee and croissants we consume on a monthly basis. We might also put a stop to internet shopping and curb the consumption of commodities. We might be more mindful of what we purchase during our weekly grocery shop, ensuring to write a list and stick to a budget (see Rule 5: Create a budget).

In case I haven't yet convinced you of the power austerity can exert, I will apply it to the outgoings/incomings chart that we created as part of our financial strategy. Below I have again boxed all those expenditures that I deem non-essential. With the sharp sword edge of austerity I shall now cut down or completely cut away those fiscal culprits that are conspiring to bring about financial ruin. At the bottom of the table I have totalled the overall saving so as to illustrate the savings that can be enjoyed with the help of our friend austerity.

Non-essential expense	Notes and saving
Mobile phone contract: £50	In truth no one in the world needs to spend this much money on a mobile phone. This contract absolutely must be reduced or cancelled. But because there are many people who are addicted to their phone (now a recognised addiction under the DSM – Diagnostic & Statistical Manual of Mental Health), we won't be so cruel as to cut it out completely. However, austerity demands that we

	severely reduce the contract and instead take out one of those smart price plans that are capped at £10.

Saving: £40 |
| **Netflix subscription: £10** | Gone! Cutting your Netflix subscription (or equivalent) will confer multiple benefits. Not only will you save ten English pounds (±£5) but also a lot of time too!

Saving: £10 |
| **Miscellaneous: £100** | Miscellaneous spending could also be called fiscal waste, for it's the type of spending that takes place when we're bored, or buying because we've been caught on a wave of consumerism.

Miscellaneous spending often takes place beneath the conscious radar and, as a consequence, most people aren't aware that they're doing it.

For example, impulse buying that £4 magazine when you're standing in the supermarket queue waiting to pay for your shopping, or abandoning all discipline and instead of just purchasing that one item off Amazon, you pile your basket high with tempting bundles. |

	Austerity necessitates that all – yes, ALL – miscellaneous spending stops. Effective immediately. **Saving: £100**
	TOTAL SAVING: £150

That's a pretty good wage for 15 minutes' work – at £10 a minute we're about on par with a premiership footballer. Now I know there will be some sceptics skim reading this who'll cast an accusing stone or two telling me that I'm being wholly unrealistic, that not everyone can reduce their phone contract, or just go cold turkey on their Netflix subscription. And who, they'll demand to know, throwing their hands out in a gesture of extreme incredulity, who in the hell wastes a hundred quid a month on stuff?

At the time of writing, a leading national newspaper reported that personal debt – that is credit card and household debt – has spiralled out of control and is now close to exceeding half a trillion pounds, which is more than double that of the pre-2008 financial crisis levels. From personal experience I know that what I've presented here is a conservative example of the disastrous state of a lot of people's financial affairs. I once worked with a person who owned over 30 pairs of trainers (the mean average price being £80), and as well as living in his overdraft, he routinely prioritised an item of fashion over putting a proper meal on the table for his children. A member of my direct family is an inveterate spender who'll never have two pennies to rub together while he's got a hole in his arse. I once asked him where his money went, what he spent it on. He nonchalantly shrugged his shoulders and without a single care in the world said, 'Stuff!'

These examples are not isolated anecdotal incidences that reside outside the realms of reality. They are reflective of a sizeable portion of the population.

Save money on household energy bills

The average household spends about £1,250 a year on heating and energy – so sayeth Ofgem, an industry regulator. This provides us with an opportunity to exercise the principles of austerity and make a monstrous saving. It is my contention – this is purely lazy supposition on my part; I haven't conducted any research to support what I'm about to say – that the vast majority of people waste energy. In fact, I would stake a sizeable pecuniary wager on the assertion that at least half of that £1,250 is spent paying for wastage, and if not gratuitous wastage, then certainly superfluous usage.

When I pop round to my one and only friend's house he's nearly always got two TVs on the go (he'll be watching one in the living room while his wife's watching one in the bedroom), or he's watching TV while pointlessly pissing about on his laptop (or phone!). In addition, there are lights on that needn't be, multiple devices charging, the dishwasher doing a job they could easily do themselves, and wherever I look I can see red standby lights dotted about the house – little energy-sucking leeches, as I call them. I've given up trying to teach him the concept of energy conservation. Yet I still find myself infuriated whenever I hear him complain about how high the 'leccy' bill is.

Of course, we shouldn't just be looking to lower our energy consumption for financial reasons. Our primary motivation ought really to be an environmental one. That is a topic of concern that resides outside the scope of this book. However, it is of secondary benefit, if saving money is your first, that any reduction in consumption you make will have a positive environmental effect – small though it is. By implementing austerity measures you stand to save considerably on your energy bills at the same time as reducing your net carbon footprint.

The following energy-reduction tips will provide you with a veritable Swiss army knife of tools and tactics to save on your utilities bill. Each tip comes accompanied with an 'estimated' yearly saving (based on Ofgem's national average). I emphasise 'estimated' because you may save less, but you might, if you're extra disciplined, save even more. Prior to implementing the tips, I recommend finding out how much you are currently spending on energy and, after the first full month of austerity, compare the difference.

Here they are:

(1) Turn off standby appliances

By turning off all of those red-eyed energy-sucking leeches you could save an average of £30 a year. Try habituating this tip by turning it into a routine. Every day, before you go to work, or at night before you climb into your coffin, make a quick sweep of the house and squish out as many of those leeches as possible.

(2) Install a smart thermostat

Smart thermostats are designed to improve the efficiency of your heating by warming only inhabited rooms. In conjunction with a smart thermostat you could also have adjustable radiator valves, which allow you to manually turn down the heat of each radiator. Of course, to install these devices you will incur an initial charge. However, sometimes you've got to speculate to accumulate. If we're looking to make savings as soon as possible so as to direct money to an overdraft or debt, then it might be worth putting this one off until you have achieved a state of financial stability. If and when you do decide to install smart thermostats and radiator valves, you could pocket a hot £75 a year.

(3) Turn down your thermostat

A cheaper and instantly implementable alternative to installing smart thermostats and radiator valves is simply to turn down the thermostat you've already got. It has been estimated that nearly half of all energy bills goes to paying for heating the home and water. By clicking down that thermostat a couple of degrees you could save £80 or more a year.

(4) Buy efficient appliances

Now this is not an excuse to rush out to Currys to replace every appliance in your kitchen. You should really only look to change an appliance when it's given up the ghost or if the infernal contraption is so old you're still feeding it coal to power it. This tip is supposed to bring about an awareness of the varying degrees of energy efficiency of different appliances. And when we learn that, for example, an A+++ fridge freezer saves us around £320 in energy bills over its lifetime compared to an A+ model, we should adjust our acquisitions accordingly.

(5) Wash clothes at a lower temperature

The washing machine, though credited with having emancipated women from domestic drudgery (so said the Cambridge economist Ha-Joon Chang), is quite possibly the single most energy-guzzling appliance in the kitchen. If you can cut your wash cycles down and wash at 30 degrees, you could reduce your electricity by as much as £5 a month.

(6) Be considerate about water usage

This one will only really resonate with people who are on a water meter. If you are on a water meter, then conserving the stuff of life could save you a pretty penny over the year. I switched to a water meter a few years back and managed to reduce my annual bill by over £100. Ways of reducing water consumption include:

- not washing your car every week, and when you do, use a bucket not a hosepipe;
- not running a tap constantly when doing the dishes or brushing your teeth;
- limiting yourself to no longer than two minutes in the shower;
- fixing leaky taps; and
- if it's yellow, let it mellow. If it's brown, flush it on down!

Ditch the car, get a pushbike!

Okay, being the realist that I am, I know for those unfortunates who have to endure a monstrous commute this suggestion is a non sequitur. Yet, it is my contention that the vast majority of people could swap their car for pedal power but don't because they're lazy and/or aren't aware of the many benefits that can be gained by using a bike. I once worked in an office with nine other people. Out of us all, I was the one who lived furthest away – a little over six miles – yet I was the only one who bothered to cycle. I say this only to substantiate my point, not for applause. I started cycling during the summer months, making the transition from four wheels to two because:

(a) I was sick of contributing to urban pollution;
(b) I utterly detest sitting in traffic and not having the freedom to bump up the curb, bypassing the queue of stressed commuters;
(c) I enjoyed the health benefits of cycling over 50 miles a week; and
(d) it saved me a ton of money!

I must admit that I did have a wobble or two when the weather got wintery. During a spate of wet and windy mornings, the rain lashing my face sore and the incessant traffic dousing me in filthy road water, I did question my sanity – that was until one of my colleagues arrived at the office late because his car had 'died' over the weekend and he had had to catch the bus. It transpired that the head gasket of his fancy BMW went pop, which cost him £1,500! 'Wow,' I remember thinking, with secret delight, 'my bike didn't even cost that much.' A few months later another colleague's car suffered a mechanical malfunction. The clutch on his quasi off-roader 'went', as he put it, costing him nearly £2,000.

Maybe this spate of automotive aberrations was a statistical anomaly compared to the average rate of breakdowns. However, no one can deny that cars guzzle more than just fuel; they guzzle money, and lots of it. When I was contemplating buying a bike, part of me needed further convincing for I got caught in a trap of focusing on the possible downsides of cycling, and I won't lie – there are many. But after crunching the numbers I was convinced. By buying a bike this is what I would no longer have to waste my money on:

- Car insurance: £135
- Road tax: £165
- MOT: £30
- Obligatory repairs to get the car through the MOT: £250 (a conservative average)
- Yearly service: £100
- Yearly valet: £25 (equivalent of an hour's wage)
- Petrol: £400 (a year)
- General wear and tear: £100

The total cost of keeping my car roadworthy equated to £1,202 a year (±£200). Of course, if your head gasket or clutch goes, that figure could more than double. Across one year of cycling I suffered a single serious mechanical fault. The 'rear mech hanger' snapped (the mech hanger is a small device that holds the rear derailleur in place). In bike terms this is the equivalent of needing a new clutch. The cost? Including labour I was out of pocket a paltry £65. Are you convinced yet?

Stop financing your own servitude

If you're still on the fence, consider that when driving you are effectively paying to work. Before I transitioned to two wheels it was costing me more than £100 a month (nearly 7.5% of my monthly net take-home pay) just to get to and from my desk.

So, before I even clocked in (metaphorically speaking), I was already out of pocket on the day's earnings. The thought of paying to work never sat well with me and it's a thought I've struggled to suppress for many years. In my eyes it's the equivalent of financing your own servitude. Imagine paying for your own chains and shackles or the slave driver's whip!

I'm not much of an anthropologist but I've noticed that few people think like this. That's why many millions of people across the nation drive to work in fancy, super-expensive cars, and many, stupider still, waste an hour's wage on overpriced coffee and confectionary every day.

At my place of employment one of those cancerous coffee shops has metastasised at the entrance to the building. When employees have made their stress-inducing commute, they invariably head straight to the coffee shop for a dopamine pick-me-up. Thus, before they even switch on the computer in preparedness for a day of drudgery, the first two hours at the desk are more or less pro bono.

Cut down on food waste

I happened to read on some obscure online forum that every year throughout Britain over 6 million tons of food finds its way into the bin. This isn't called the age of waste for nothing! The anonymous Joe who posted that didn't bother to calculate how many people 6 million tons of food could feed, but I bet it's a lot. Nourishment and grotesque waste aside – few people, when throwing food in the bin, stop to think about the agricultural and industrial effort expended to produce it – I would like to draw your attention to the financial cost of food waste.

According to WRAP (the Waste and Resources Action Programme charity), over £30 million worth of lettuce and strawberries are wasted annually. That's more than the GDP of North Korea – wasted on rabbit food and an insignificant berry! And these are quite possibly two of the lightest foods you can find on the supermarket shelves. So if £30,000,000 is being wasted on two foods that comprise a mere fraction of the 6 million tons wasted, how much money, I wonder, is wasted in total? Well, after five exasperating minutes of searching the first web pages that popped up when I typed 'food wastage' into the search engine, I failed to find much in the way of a credible source. However, some estimates pitched the cost of that 6 million tons of food wastage as high as £20 billion. Hell, if you could convert that into a net worth, you'd land yourself on the coveted Forbes Rich List – and beneath you on that lofty ladder, clambering desperately for another rung, would be many an envious oil baron, Russian oligarch, tech tycoon and investment icon.

But while we can't nab the entire pie, we can save a few crumbs. If the average UK household bins about £500 in wasted food a year (a little over £40 a month),[4] there are potential savings to be made. By being more mindful of the food we buy, the meals we plan to cook and the way in which we prepare those meals, we stand to shave a substantial sum off our weekly shop. Here are two simple ways of reducing food wastage.

(1) Make meals in batches

By batching our meals – that is, cooking more than we plan to consume at the initial sitting – you can either enjoy an easy meal the following evening or freeze the leftovers for another day.

(2) Formulate a weekly meal plan

Every Saturday morning my significant other and I decide what we're going to eat the following week. Once we've settled on a menu, we create a list of food items we'll need from the market. When we do this, we ensure to stay within a pre-specified budget of £50 – which we are not, under any circumstances, allowed to exceed (see **Rule 5: Create a Budget**). Over the years I have found this to be one of the best ways to reduce food waste.

Making do with what you've got

Generalities or sweeping statements are a sign of intellectual laziness; they're the equivalent of dropping a bomb to kill one person when a single bullet would have done the job. Nasty metaphor I know. But aren't we all guilty of having and wanting

---

[4] 'Reports – food waste from all sectors', *WRAP*. www.wrap.org.uk/content/all-sectors. Last accessed 6 November 2020.

far more than we need? Seneca, the wise Roman and poster boy of Stoicism, the philosophy of practising asceticism and preparing to die, said as much 2000 years ago.

> Any man who does not think that what he has is more than ample is an unhappy man, even if he is the master of the whole world (Letter IX).

He has much more to say on the matter of what we might today call frugality or austerity. Seneca's prevailing premise has much merit – to wit, we can enjoy a full and contented life while subsisting on the bare essentials.

> If you shape your life according to nature, you will never be poor; if according to people's opinions, you will never be rich (Letter XVI).

Why? you may well ask. Because opinions, wishing and wanting are without limit whereas our basic needs are few.

Today, this philosophy goes by another name: minimalism (not to be confused with *nihil*ism). Generally considered the art of subsisting off very little, minimalism, much like austerity, requires that you reduce not only how much stuff you possess but also how much you consume.

I'm reminded of a time a number of years ago when a work colleague walked into the office huffing and puffing as he struggled to carry four obese bin liners. He dumped them disdainfully beside his desk and flounced back into his chair where he took a moment to catch his breath and dab at the sweat trickling down his greasy brow. I asked him what was in the bags, adding that I hoped it wasn't his ex-girlfriend. He leaned forward, not without considerable effort, untied one of the bags and spilled its viscera over the floor. Clothes, heaps and heaps of clothes! I wandered over to inspect them, most of which sported designer labels and looked to be unworn. I asked what he planned to do with them, to which he said, 'Bin 'em, or, if I can be bothered, cart them down to the local charity shop.' A moment later he invited me to take as many and as much as I pleased. I thanked him for his generous offer but politely declined on account of having a sufficiently furnished wardrobe already. After venting a shrill and incredulous laugh he said, 'You can never have enough clothes!' I pointed at the four bags stuffed full of contradiction.

After a quick rifle through his throwaways I got to calculating the cost of all these clothes and arrived at an eye-popping estimate of £2,000 (±10%). When I put this to him he shrugged his shoulders and said, 'So.' I was taken aback by his nonchalant response. I asked him did he not think it was a waste of money. He shook his head, 'No – plus, you've got to spend your money on something.' Acknowledging his trite maxim I enquired why he was throwing so many clothes away. 'Because I've bought a load of new stuff and no longer have the space.'

Now this attitude and show of decadent excess and wastage was no surprise coming from an extreme extrovert who thought little of wasting a week's wage on a single night out on the town. However, although he was a professional pedagogue who earned about five grand over the national yearly average, he quite literally did not have a pot to piss in. He lived with his parents at an age when most have long since fled the nest; for the five years that I knew him he never once climbed out of his overdraft; and he didn't have a single solitary cent in savings.

It is from people like this that we can learn a lesson. Remember: the intelligent person learns from their own mistakes whereas the philosopher learns from the mistakes of others. The protagonist of my tale perfectly exemplifies where wanting more than we need can lead, viz. financial destitution. And he is by no means an exception. There are millions of people across the country who are trapped in a cycle of base consumerism – and I bet most of them don't even realise it. By curbing excessive spending and exercising more awareness of our purchasing habits, most of us stand to make significant savings.

As for those four bags of clothes, what was their fate? Well, as you have probably already guessed, they didn't find their way to a charity shop. Instead they were discarded in a Biffa bin!

I'll conclude my thoughts on austerity with some more of Seneca's sagacious words:

> Natural desires are limited; but those which spring from false opinion can have no stopping-point. The false has no limits. When you are travelling on a road, there must be an end; but when astray, your wanderings are limitless. Recall your steps, therefore, from idle things, and when you would know whether that which you seek is based upon a natural or upon a misleading desire, consider whether it can stop at any definite point. If you find, after having travelled far, that there is a more distant goal always in view, you may be sure that this condition is contrary to nature.
> *Letters From A Stoic* – Letter XVI

Conclusion

So here ends our study of the principles of financial strategy and austerity and the many fascinating ways that they can be applied. I feel it necessary to conclude this section with a few remarks regarding the need to exercise caution when implementing austerity measures.

Although it might be hard to believe right now, beware – austerity can become quite addictive. There is a feel-good sensation that naturally comes from reducing consumption and that is only compounded when we start to see those savings come pouring in. My advice is to mix austerity with Aristotelian moderation – that is, enjoy a significant reduction in your necessary outgoings but not so much that you start living like Brand, that pitiful priest in Ibsen's play.

It's now over to you. In the space provided below, I offer you the opportunity to have a go at fashioning your own strategy of how you plan to improve your financial situation. It might help to make use of the principles of strategy – identify your destination and then plan a route to get there. Before you get started, I'll leave you with an apropos sagacious one-liner from St. Jean-Baptiste-Marie Vianney:

On this path, it is only the first step that counts.

My Financial Amelioration Strategy

The Rules

In this section, we're going to look in detail at my top ten rules for whipping your finances into shape. I regard them as rules, as opposed to tips, tricks and tools, for the simple fact that they ought to be rigidly enforced – and if broken accompanied with severe punitive punishment; such as a fine, community service or house arrest.

The reason why they should be so strictly observed is because they are designed to ensure safe financial practices. Much the same way as laws are supposed to support the structural integrity of society, making it a safer place for its citizens, the rules that are soon to follow can do the same for your finances – if, of course, they are treated with equal respect.

A quick word on how to implement them. It would be an act of folly to 'promulgate' rules in multiples. To do so would probably result in transgression which would inevitably lead to despondency and slipping back into unhealthy money management practices. You stand a greater chance of avoiding these undesirable outcomes if you implement one rule at a time.

But once ratified, so to speak, the rule should not be repealed for a minimum of three months. Why? Because little to no noticeable financial benefit will be enjoyed if you vacillate from one rule to another without giving it time to work its magic. So, implement a rule for three months, and if after that time it has made a positive difference to your financial life, maintain it and move on. If it doesn't yield the desired results, discard it and try another. In short, get experimental.

Rule 1: Spend Half, Save Half (aka the 50/50 maxim)

A wise man once said to me, 'Adam, when it comes to money management, my advice is always this: after you've paid the bills, save half and spend half.' Good, simple, wholesome advice I think you would agree. And if followed, it will safeguard you against debt, overdrafts and other financial unpleasantness. Now the wise man who so kindly imparted the above sagacious financial advice wasn't merely echoing ancestral wisdom. He was a financial advisor by profession who retired to a life of ease and luxury before hitting fifty. What he told me was the distillation and consolidation of years of experience helping financial misfits better manage their money. During that time he identified one critical mistake made by the majority of his clients. The mistake? A failure to set aside a sum of their earnings each month for savings. My financial advisor friend later coined this 50/50 maxim.

Though seemingly self-explanatory, and it indubitably is, I'll explain this rule anyway just to give you an idea of how your monthly income might be divided so as to leave some spare for a savings account.

Say you earn £1,500 per calendar month (this sum is not arbitrary, it is relative to the purported national average) and your necessary outgoings (bills) are half that – £750. With the remaining £750 you would be wise to split that in half again (£375) and deposit it in a savings account (see **Rule 2: Structure Your Accounts**). If this were possible for you to do, over the course of the year you would save over £4,000 (disbarring any unforeseen pecuniary pit-holes).

Now it's your turn to do your sums.

	Incoming	Outgoing
Monthly income (after tax)	£	
Mortgage		£
Utilities (combined)		£
Car insurance		£
Car running costs		£
Home/contents insurance		£
Monthly groceries (estimated)		£
Other		£
Other		£
Other		£
Other		£
Other		£
Outgoings total		**£**
Cash remaining when outgoings are subtracted from incomings	£	
50% savings		**50% spending**
£		£

For its simplicity alone the 50/50 maxim is a money management marvel. It can be comprehended by most anyone and implemented effectively immediately. Moreover, the 50/50 maxim is not so Machiavellian that it makes you feel as though you are under the tyrannical rule of an oppressive dictator. After all, this rule allows you to spend some of your hard-earned cash, which is not the case when you're observing a spending fast or implementing austerity measures. In this sense the 50/50 maxim is comparatively liberal.

If you were to follow this one rule, and follow it resolutely, never would you be without a financial safety net, no matter how small your 50% saving contribution was. Which is more than can be said for millions of UK citizens. A recently published report into the state of the nation's financial health showed that between 15% and 20% of British people eligible to work haven't a single penny in savings, and 1 in 3 have less than £800.[1] These figures could be even more dire if savings were offset against personal debt. This is a failing of the report. Of those people who have a small sum in savings, how many are carrying credit card debt, financing an overdraft deficit or servicing a car loan? If a person has £800 in savings but is simultaneously saddled with a £1,500 credit card repayment, they are in reality £700 in debt.

By applying the spend half, save half rule you will always be in the category of financially sensible people who have a rainy-day reserve.

Rule 2: Structure Your Accounts

Establishing a logically organised accounting system is a money management must. The person whose accounts are in disarray is likely to be plagued with a plethora of pecuniary problems ranging from sudden and unexpected droughts to debilitating

---

[1] Matthew Boyle, 'Savings statistics: Average savings in the UK 2020.' 13 August 2020. *Finder* website. https://www.finder.com/uk/saving-statistics. Last accessed 9 November 2020.

debt. If your accounts are disorganised – or don't exist! – Rule 2 will show you to set up and structure three savings accounts (SA) so that you can start building a strong financial fortress.

The first savings account (SA 1), an ISA maybe, or some other long-term investment account, is the fail-safe. This is only to be accessed if an HM Revenue and Customs officer is pulling on a pair of latex gloves (Vaseline not optional I'm afraid), or two 6'6" meatheads are kicking down your door. Other than these two undesirable eventualities SA 1 is the 'nest egg'.

As we'll see later on – it's a recurrent theme throughout – psychology plays a massive part when it comes to managing one's money. Here's an example. Many years ago an American banker created a zero-interest Christmas savers account. This was, amongst the fraternity, ridiculed – who would be stupid enough to put their money into an account that offered zero interest? However, there was one minor difference with this account: the holder could not draw out their money until the month of December. How many people have started off with the good intentions of saving for something only to succumb to the temptation of dipping into the honeypot early?

Saving is a game of wit and discipline. The majority of people recognise that they lack the discipline, so in this instance they used their wit. By putting money into an account from which withdrawals were prohibited, they played the game of psychology – and there isn't necessarily anything wrong with this if it achieves the required results. Consequently, because of the inherent flaw in Homo *sapiens*' willpower, the Christmas savers account was a huge hit.

So, with this in mind, when setting up SA1 it might be wise to look for a long-term fixed account – 3 to 5 years. Because it's fixed-term, withdrawals will be met with penalties – usually proportional to the loss of the projected interest rates over the remaining investment period.

The second savings account (SA 2) is to be accessed when a big spend is necessary or when encountering one of those blind bends on the road of life. I'll give you an example of when a second savings account can come in handy and why it is important to have something like this in place. A friend of mine, who does not heed advice and is completely inept when it comes to managing his money, took his car to the garage for a routine MOT. They called him up after a couple of hours and told him that, in short, his engine was shot. Shot! 'What do you mean shot?' he asked. Unfixable and not legally roadworthy is apparently what 'shot' means. He was left with only one viable option: weigh his old car in for scrap and buy a new one. Because he had no savings he could not buy from a private seller – that would require liquid cash and he was as dry as the Sahara – he was therefore forced to take out finance with a dealership. His new second-hand car came with no mod cons, just a fixed-term 17.5% interest rate. (I did a bit of maths for him and it transpired that, over the term of the loan, he would have to pay roughly an additional £650!)

If, however, my friend had heeded the first rule (see **Rule 1: Spend Half, Save Half (aka the 50/50 maxim)**) and split his savings across three accounts (or one account!), it's likely that he'd have amassed enough to afford – at the very least – a cheap runaround.

54

The third savings account (SA 3) is for the finer things in life: holidays, a material want, a meal out, a decadent item of dress, etc., etc. *ad infinitum.*

Now, bringing to mind Rule 1 (the 50/50 maxim), I am going to give you an idea of how you might direct the flow of your 'save half' funds into the three SAs. However, this can be tailored to suit your current financial situation. Remember, though, if your earnings prohibit a three-tier system you can always drop down to two or even one – just so long as something is being squirrelled away.

So, going back to the example discussed under Rule 1, we were left with a figure of £375 that *must* be directed into savings. Because I like to keep things nice and simple I'd divide that sum as follows: £200 into SA 1; £100 into SA 2; and £75 into SA 3. If this system were rigidly adhered to, after one year here's what the three savings accounts would look like:

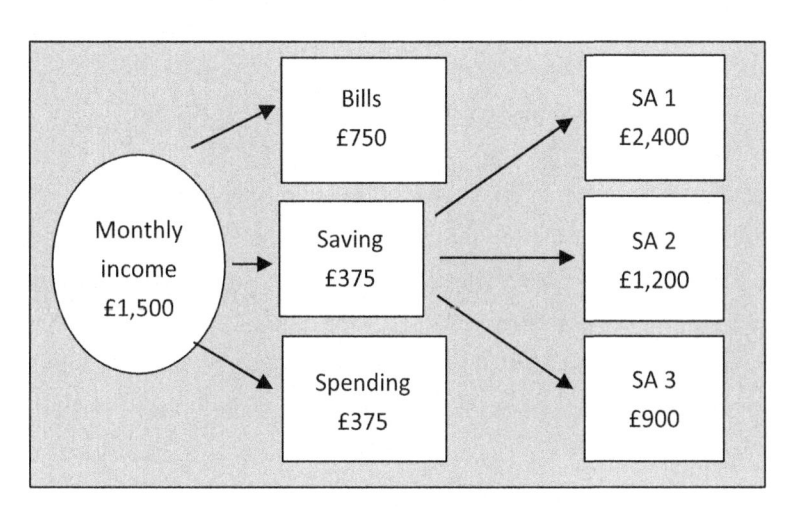

Monthly income £1,500	Bills £750	SA 1 £2,400
	Saving £375	SA 2 £1,200
	Spending £375	SA 3 £900

That gives a savings grand total of £4,500!

And to think, that's just from saving half of half of what's left over after fattening the wolves. The power of accumulation (see **Tip 4: The Law of Incremental Accumulation**) is evident in the numbers.

Rule 3: Ask Yourself These Three Important Questions

My momma always said to me, 'Son, before buying anything, ask yourself these three questions,' (at this point, holding her right hand in front of my face, she'd flick out a finger every time she fired off a question) 'firstly: can I afford it? Secondly: do I need it? Thirdly: do I want it? If you can answer "Yes" to two out of three, then get it!'

Ah, don't you just love ancestral wisdom, even if it is a crock of horseshit? Yet even though we know intuitively it's a load of rubbish, why is it so hard to question? And why does it stick with us for so long?

My grandma used to tell me that if I made mocking faces my features would forever freeze in those ghastly gargoyle-like contortions and I'd consequently die a virgin. My older brother loved to tell me that I'd go blind if I masturbated. Scared stiff (no pun intended) of both eventualities, I've abstained for thirty long years from pulling faces and the other thing. In all that time I've never questioned the causal relationship between face-pulling and ugliness and self-gratification and macular degeneration. Thankfully, this is not the case with my mother's advice. But I've noticed that her logic was oh so very slightly flawed. Allow me to explain.

The aim of this rule is to encourage you to pause before parting with your cash (indeed, just becoming more consciously aware of your spending habits can exert a dramatic impact on superfluous spending). But the rule as it presently stands doesn't prevent you from slipping over the precipice and toppling down a cliff into a chasm of debt. For example, you might want to buy the thing so badly that you convince yourself that you need it, irrespective of whether or not you have the money. This is the flaw to which I previously alluded and it must be rectified.

If we make one small amendment to my mother's shrewd spending advice it can be transformed into a bulletproof, Teflon-coated, impenetrable jacket of financial security. And the amendment? Simply this: the first question must *always* be asked first and *always* answered in the affirmative. Q2 and Q3 cannot veto Q1 by majority – this is not a democracy; it's a dictatorship governed by the omnipotent Q1.

So when standing in front of a shop window glaring covetously at that super sleek pair of sneakers, you should ask yourself those three questions: Q1) Can I afford them? Q2) Do I need them? Q3) Do I want them?

If you cannot honestly and unequivocally answer Q1 with a resounding 'Yes', you are forbidden from making that purchase.

Rule 4: Delay Gratification

Human beings have the capacity to learn to want almost any conceivable material object. Given, then, the emergence of a modern industrial culture capable of producing almost anything, the time is ripe for opening the storehouse of infinite need! ... It is the modern Pandora's box, and its plagues are loose upon the world.

Jules Henry

This is a tough one, there's no denying it, and it can only work if you struggle and strive to cultivate self-discipline. In saying that, though, we can use some pretty subtle psychological tricks to curb spending and delay gratification.

What Jules Henry said is true – there has not been a period of time throughout all human history when material things were as abundant and more readily available to buy as they are today. This accounts for why the average person has vastly more than they need and why personal debt is on the increase – amongst many other socially undesirable vices. The capitalists have cottoned on to the seemingly inherent human inability to say NO! May I remind you that the collapse of the Western world's economic system in 2008 was precipitated by people taking on mortgages that they could not financially support. Coupled with the insatiable greed of lenders and what do you get? An economic apocalypse and years of austerity, retrenchment and social misery. And what's the root cause? Simply people's inability to delay gratification, to say to themselves, 'At the moment I can't afford to support a mortgage of this size, so I'll look for a smaller property that's within my financial means.'

The new money-trap on the block is lease cars. At the time of writing, between 85% and 91% of all cars on British roads are in some way financed through a third-party lender. In the past, the process of buying a car required the perspective buyer to have the capital to cover the sale price. If you walked into a showroom and the car you wanted cost £10,000, then you needed that much money – unless you could haggle the salesperson down. The problem with this method is that, because people tend to be quite poor at saving, few had the capital to finance the purchase. Thus few cars were sold. This presented car manufacturers with a conundrum: how could they increase sales in a market where only a fraction of consumers could afford their product. And the answer they came up with? Buy now, pay later! (Or buy now and make small repayments for the next 10 years.) Today, thanks to the lease initiative, many people are effectively burdened with a second mortgage – one for the home and another for their car. Nowadays, for two to three hundred pounds a month (discounting the initial purchase deposit), you could be at the wheel of a top-of-the-range brand-spanking new motor.

I used to car share with someone who 'owned' one of these lease cars. He didn't have the financial means to buy a new car, so instead he settled for parting with a week's wages to support the illusory image of success. The best part of it was that, because there was a mileage cap on the car that would result in a fine were it exceeded, he was forced to park his shiny penis extension on my drive for two weeks out of every month. I brought this home to him with some crude calculations. If he didn't exceed the mileage quota, the car was costing him £300 every month (not including general running costs – but we'll ignore this). If the car was not being used for two weeks out of the month, that meant he was paying the car dealership £150 for the privilege of parking it. Of every two months at work one whole week was spent earning the money to finance a car that he could only use half the time. That's crazy!

After our little chat, which from the outset I could tell was not welcomed, I told him to return that bottomless pit on wheels to the nefarious dealership and offered to drive him in my old banger, worth about £125 at the time; all he had to do was pay one week's petrol every month. If he took up my offer, he'd save £280 a month and in ten months he'd have a cool £2,800 in his back pocket – which, I think you'll agree, would cover the cost of a pretty nice second-hand runaround. But did he heed my advice? Did he take up my magnanimous offer? I think you know the answer to those questions. Instead, he opted to support a corrupt financial system and prop up a false economy.

So, getting back to the methods one can use to delay gratification, you could use the one I've just elucidated. Play the waiting game and save those pennies. This, though, isn't to everyone's taste. It's hard to say 'No', especially when companies make it so easy for us to say 'Yes'.

One simple way I use to curb spending is to turn an electronic transaction into a physical one by drawing out the cash first. Paying on a credit card, or over the internet, is easy, primarily because:

> (a) you don't make a physical transaction – parting with a fiscal medium such as money, a tangible expression of your labour time, can be a sobering, even thought-provoking experience (and it can more acutely evoke the dreaded 'buyer's remorse' or the 'buyer's blues'); and
> (b) it's an impersonal approach to procuring material wants – swiping a piece of plastic or clicking a couple of buttons requires little to no thought.

Spending money has never been so easy

Have you noticed how companies are making it ever easier for us to part with our hard-earned money? What costs hours, days, weeks, months and sometimes years to earn can be spent in seconds. We now have contactless cards where you merely have to suspend your card over a chip-and-pin device to make a payment. In the click of a finger anything from a few pennies to £45 can be sucked out of your account.

Internet companies do their utmost to encourage customers to open an account with them. To open an account you're required to input your debit/credit card details and other personal information. By doing this the company removes any barriers that may slow or inhibit the customer from making a purchase. In a few quick clicks the customer can fill their basket to the brim with overpriced commodities and pay for them without so much as a thought.

One thing you should remember – these effortless forms of financial transaction have not been created for the good of humanity. Contactless payment was not conceived by a benevolent financier to make our lives easier. The aim is only and always to speed up the flow of cash from your pocket to their coffers.

But you can't blame businesses; that's just their nature – just like it's the nature of a leech to latch on, sink its teeth into your flesh and suck! Consequently, if you want to avoid getting drained dry, you must take responsibility and safeguard yourself. One simple method of doing this is to pay, where possible, with cash. As for internet shopping, don't; close your accounts.

A few years back I wanted to treat myself to a nice watch. What mental malfunction triggered this desire I can't say. The timepiece, as they are called by pretentious horologists, cost £2,000, and after asking myself the three questions (see **Rule 3**) I decided to go ahead with this singularly stupid splurge. Instead of purchasing the watch online I thought it might be nice to go to the shop and browse a little before making my purchase. Also, I could try it on for size and strike a couple of James Bond-style poses. After I withdrew £2,000 cash at the bank, I made the mile-long walk to the watch shop. That hefty wad in my bulging pocket, rubbing against my outer thigh, made its presence felt every step of the way. Doubt began to creep in. I reached into my pocket and began to finger the cash. A bout of nervousness triggered an adrenaline dump; butterflies suddenly congregated in my stomach and began fluttering about erratically. Was I going to burgle the shop or buy something from it? The lick of sweat across my brow, my greasy palms and mounting anxiety made it hard to determine what was going on.

Suffice to say I never reached the shop. Instead, I found myself back at the bank re-depositing £2,000 into my account, much to the irritation of the disgruntled cashier who'd previously counted it out for me. I've since made do with my old watch, and though it is less than 1% of the price of the watch I almost bought, it tells the time perfectly. Moral of the story: if there is a margin of doubt in your mind before making a purchase, draw the cash out – it works for me 95% of the time.

Some delay tactics you could employ:

- Take a cold shower.
- Run through the purchase with your mum. If yours is anything like mine, she will discourage you with a single disapproving look.
- Reason it out logically: do I really need this thing? Will it really improve my life? Can I do without it?
- Hide or destroy all means and methods of making payment. Cut your debit/credit card in two, telling yourself as you do that if you still want to buy the thing when the new card arrives in a week's time, you'll get it! Chances are, the desire will have well worn off by then.

A great tactic I use to deter spending is to follow the chain of production back to its route source and then work out how much profit the producer/retailer is making. I once read a report in a national newspaper that brought this home. After Christmas 2015, investigators exposed the shocking price hike of a knitted toy penguin. Production costs for manufacturing this cuddly toy were 25p. After a bump in price from manufacturer to distributor, the high-street retailer felt it fair to sell each individual toy at a whopping ... wait for it ... £95! (It is for this reason that I obstinately refuse to buy anything over the Christmas period.) I grow incensed at the idea of some fat cat capitalist rolling in cash at my expense (I can see him rubbing his greasy paws together while laughing at my stupidity). However, because I've become a dab hand at delaying gratification, I no longer make purchases that I'll later regret, thus I no longer contribute to keeping the capitalists in caviar.

Rule 5: Create a Budget

Creating a budget is a simple and extremely effective way to manage your money. As penny-pinching ideas go it's probably one of the oldest in the book. People have been budgeting in some form or another for thousands of years. The ancient Egyptians and Greeks, after harvesting crops at the end of the summer, used to store the fruits of their labour in huge purpose-built wooden containers and apportion weekly quantities to ensure that it lasted over the lean winter months. It's our capacity to budget, to allocate a portion of our present wealth to be used in the future, that gives us the edge over the caprices of fortune and enables us to weather the hard times when there's a dearth in resources.

In addition, when we enforce a budget we inadvertently erect boundaries and walls which, like the walls of a dam, prevent money from draining away. The habitual budgeter shares many striking similarities with the industrious beaver; both build indomitable structures – one psychological the other physical – that prohibit the depletion of precious resources.

At its essence financial budgeting is when we set aside a fixed sum of money that we are to subsist on for an allotted period of time. During that time, however long it may be, we must exercise the necessary discipline to make sure we don't exceed our budget cap. For example, if you saved up, say, £1,000 spending money for a ten-day holiday, you might, if you were sensible, set yourself a budget of £100 a day. By doing this, by fixing that specific sum and sticking to it for the ten days, you will not find yourself at the end of your sunny vacation panhandling change to pay for your last supper.

I once made this mistake during a five-week holiday in Thailand. As a consequence of living it up a little too large, and constantly overshooting my daily budget, I somehow frittered away five weeks worth of spending money in four. This led to the embarrassing situation of having to phone home to ask Mum if she could transfer a couple of hundred quid into my account. Lesson learned, right? Wrong! In a few days I'd spent every last penny of the £200 lifeline my mum had magnanimously thrown me and found myself at the airport unable to foot the £30 visa extension charge. Thankfully a friend hadn't been so reckless with his money and was able to finance my way through customs.

That, by the way, is an example of how *not* to budget.

Below are a couple of examples of how *to* budget. It is not necessary to list numerous budgeting scenarios because really the underlying principle is the same irrespective of the financial situation.

Example 1
At the weekend, to prevent runaway spending, I limit myself to £50. Come Saturday morning I mosey on down to the local cash machine and withdraw £50, then promptly hide my debit card from myself. This is to last me over the weekend and if it doesn't, if I'm foolish and overspend, then ... well, tough! I go without and

that's that. Inevitably, though, I'll have been quite conservative, thus enabling me to deposit a tenner or two into one of my secret-stash tins (see **Tip 2** in Tips, Tricks and Tools).

Why do I use cash instead of plastic? For budgeting purposes cash trumps plastic every time for two reasons. Firstly it's finite – when you blow all your cash that's it, it's gone! You can't spend more than you've got in your pocket and, importantly, you can't dip into your overdraft. Secondly, it's physical. When you withdraw cash from an ATM and hold it in your hands, you quickly form a relationship with it. That money represents the sweet fruits of your hard labour, therefore it is not to be mindlessly and carelessly squandered (see my earlier story about the £2,000 watch). When you spend cash, you can literally see it dwindle away. Plastic, much like a blow-up doll, is impersonal and open to abuse.

Example 2
Every year across the UK billions of pounds worth of leftover food is chucked in the bin. Why? Because the majority of shoppers fail to adequately estimate how much food they'll need to last them for the week.

Writing a shopping list in accordance with a week's worth of pre-planned meals, and taking a limited sum of money to the supermarket will guarantee that (a) you buy what you need to last the week; and (b) you don't overspend by buying items that aren't on your list.

Of course, if you only take cash, then you are completely prevented from breaching your budget. Also if, like me, you have a tendency to break as easily as a warm Kit Kat, I advise you not to go shopping on an empty stomach. That is a sure-fire way to find yourself double-dipping on delicacies (aka confectioneries), or getting caught banqueting on the grapes while you play supermarket sweep.

Budgeting is as old as its nemesis, usury – lending with exorbitant interest rates. Thankfully, though, the concept is not complicated – hell, I used to budget my weekly pocket money (still do). To budget well all you need to do is make sure you set aside a specific sum (preferably in cash), marginally more than necessary, and quite simply stay within the safe confines of that fiscal fence. Making a habit of this behaviour will help you to develop monetary discipline while enhancing your sensitivity to spending practices. It is my belief that regimented routine reduces the risk of financial deviation.

Four steps to establishing a budget
Step 1: Work out how much money you need.

Before you decide the size of your budget you must first calculate what expenses it is expected to cover. Neglecting to figure out how much is needed to finance the weekly shop or weekend vacation is the most common mistake people make when budgeting. Let's consider this in relation to the example of the ten-day holiday. Prior to going on holiday, perhaps even as much as a year in advance, you would consider how much each day will cost. This cost would encompass such expenses as food, treats, travel and activities. Once you have arrived at an accurate daily allowance you would be wise to increase the figure by at least 10% to cover for emergencies or unexpected expenditure.

Step 2: Decide the length of time the budget is to cover.

Staying with the example above, once you have established the average daily cost of being on holiday, it would now be prudent to calculate the total spending money required for the entire ten days. To arrive at the total you would simply multiply the daily cost by the number of days that your holiday is scheduled to last for.

Step 3: Allocate the funds.

Once you know how much is needed and how long it's needed for, you must allocate the necessary funds. This can either be achieved through saving, just as you did for the holiday itself, or by setting aside a specific portion of your monthly income.

Step 4: Exercise budgetary discipline.

This process is all for naught if you're incapable of maintaining the discipline required to stop yourself from exceeding your budget. Of all the steps, this is the one I imagine the majority of people will struggle with the most. But overcoming wavering willpower isn't as difficult as it is often made out to be. I find the most effective weapon when battling weak discipline is to use tactical intelligence. If you were soon to jet off to a sun-soaked stretch of the Mediterranean coastline for ten days but were worried that your spending money will likely be squandered in half that time, how might you overcome this potentially ruinous problem? It's quite simple really. If you split your spending money into daily allocations and place it into its own clearly labelled container (such as a plastic money bag), you will significantly decrease the likelihood of exceeding your budget.

Rule 6: Cut the Credit Cards

Warren Buffett, probably the single most successful investor in human history, gave this advice when speaking about the financial future of American youth: 'Avoid credit cards. Forget about them. You can't make progress in your financial life ... if you run up credit card debt.' He then went on to say that even though he has large investments in credit companies, he still advises people to steer clear.[2]

Who is Warren Buffett and why does his advice matter? At the age of twelve he started to read books on investment strategies. Less than two years later he'd read every book in the local library and saved ten thousand dollars by working multiple jobs. He then invested this money (and his many hours of learning) in various companies, built up his own investment business – Berkshire Hathaway – and at the height of his career was purportedly worth sixty billion US dollars.

Why then, if credit cards are known financial deathtraps, do people still use them? The inability to delay gratification is probably the first reason on the list (see **Rule 4: Delay Gratification**): I want that thing now but I can't afford it ... credit card! A second reason is because those with no savings have no other way of dealing with the capricious hand of fate: my car has just blown up and I have no savings to get another one ... credit card! Apart from these two reasons it's hard to see why anyone

---

[2] Warren Buffet, 'How to Stay Out of Debt – Financial Future of American Youth' (1999). *YouTube.* https://www.youtube.com/watch?v=IvveZr0D_9Y. Last accessed 10 November 2020.

would be foolish enough to fall into this financial abyss. Lots of people do, though.

Avoid using credit cards for the following:
- **Everyday purchases.** Whether you're going out for a meal, filling up the car or adorning your wardrobe with another garment, the general consensus from independent financial advisors across the board is to use your own money, not the bank's. Amassing debt on credit cards is a dangerous habit and it is one that could lead you straight into the doldrums of financial and emotional ruin. Credit card companies make it very easy for you to spend *their* money. To be sure, this is not done out of the goodness of their hearts to help you. They want to keep feeding you rope so that eventually you'll end up hanging yourself on the end of a fixed-term interest repayment penalty. And nationally there are millions swinging on the scaffold. To sum up: when making general, everyday purchases use your own money.
- **Cash withdrawals.** A person who withdraws cash on a credit card is asking – nay! *begging* – for trouble. The standard transaction fee for cash withdrawals is 24% – that's a charge of 24p for every single pound withdrawn! Why are cash transaction fees so high? It's probably to do with the bank or lender trying to discourage you, the borrower, from doing what they are doing – to wit, engaging in leech-like money-lending practices. If no financial charge was incurred when withdrawing cash on a credit card, it wouldn't take long for someone to realise that they could lend the bank's money to a third-party borrower with interest added. Theoretically you could still

do this, but you'd have to find someone desperate enough to borrow money above a 24% interest rate.

So when is it okay to use a credit card?

1) When you are going to make a substantial purchase where it makes more sense to use the bank's money rather than your own.

Say, by way of hypothetical example, I was going to acquire a new guitar that cost £3,000. I've got that much in Savings Account 1 (see **Rule 2: Structure Your Accounts**), but it's earning me interest and I stand to lose money if I withdraw it. What do I do in this instance? Well, I desperately need the guitar; my life depends on it. Now I've conned myself and pacified my soul, I'll have to rationalise the acquisition in accordance with the three questions (see **Rule 3: Ask Yourself These Three Important Questions**). All good on that score. The next logical step is to take out a credit card with a 0% interest rate for no less than a year and pay it back slowly. I get my guitar and keep my money that's earning interest. All I have to do is make sure that I am disciplined enough to maintain the monthly repayments – which, of course, I have budgeted for before making the purchase.

2) When paying for products or services where you could potentially lose your money, such as internet purchases, holidays, spending on holiday, etc.

It is not uncommon to hear stories of people who made a purchase online from a phoney, non-existent company, or who booked a holiday only to find out at the boarding desk that the holiday company has gone bust! In those two incidences the unfortunate customer would very likely find themselves without

71

a leg to stand on when trying to get their money back. This is perhaps one of the few occasions when a credit card comes in handy, as it would be the bank – for a change – being robbed, not the customer.

3) To amass points with purchasing power, air miles and/or to acquire any other carrot that credit card companies dangle to encourage spending.
If used sensibly, credit cards can confer some consumer benefits; much the way loyalty cards can. By making regular purchases it is possible to amass points which can be converted into an acquisition. I know someone who paid for an entire holiday, flights and all, with their credit card points – but they had been collecting them for a number of years. Though this is perfectly above board, arguably sensible even, it is imperative to exercise caution and restraint for credit cards, in my opinion, are as dangerous as class A drugs. When using them in this way it would be wise to remain within a strict budget – say £50 per month – and set up a direct debit of the same amount to clear the balance. In short, stay disciplined and automate.

The number one rule to abide by when using credit cards is this: **only ever use a credit card if – IF! – you have the money to offset the purchase amount**.

What I mean by this is: if you spend two, three, four or ten grand on a credit card, make sure that you have two, three, four or ten grand in an account somewhere. Why? Because if you miscalculate the budgeting of repayments, or get savaged by one of life's unforeseen chimeras, you can settle the balance before incurring interest charges.

72

I've got an apropos story of this happening to someone who racked up debt on store cards. She foolishly bit off more than she could chew and missed a fixed repayment. As a result she was forcibly removed from her 0% interest rate and placed on one close to 25%. If she serviced the debt at the stipulated minimum amount on this interest rate, she would, over the course of nine years (yes, *nine* years), have paid back over five times the original sum. She'd very nearly taken out a mortgage on clothes and other pointless consumables. Eventually, when this burden became too great to carry alone, she solicited support from her father.

Dad, a financial advisor (the same one who bequeathed me with the 50/50 maxim), did what good parents should do – that is, precisely nothing. 'It's your mess, you clean it up.' His refusal to interfere, though easy to misconstrue as patriarchal belligerence, was in fact a calculated attempt to imbue his daughter with autonomy over her own financial future. This stopped the day she broke down in front of him, a blubbering wreck. When it all finally got too much, when she realised that she could not get herself out of the hole she'd unwittingly tumbled into, she pleaded for help. Her dad said he would, of course – but only under one condition: that she sign over power of attorney, giving him complete control over all of her finances, thus allowing him to dictate her spending habits. Desperation forced her to concede to this authoritarian approach. But alas! In less than a year he'd paid off all her debt(s), built up a substantial amount in savings while providing her with enough disposable cash to enjoy life. How did he do this? Firstly, he restructured her accounts and followed them up with a barrage of bulletproof budgets. He then devised a series of automated saving streams after curtailing all superfluous spending. Finally, he focused her remaining income on the primary problem. Suffice to say, after this horrendous ordeal, she never touched a credit card again. She learned a valuable lesson from this expensive mistake.

Moral: clever people learn from their mistakes, philosophers learn from the mistakes of others.

To consolidate or not to consolidate; that is the question

> The motive to credit is the hope of advantage. Commerce can never be at a stop while one man wants what another can supply; and credit will never be denied while it is likely to be repaid with profit.
>
> Dr Samuel Johnson

Sometimes it makes sense to put all your eggs in one basket – in both a literal and a metaphorical sense. By having all your real eggs in one place, as opposed to scattered about, you know exactly where they are and precisely how many you've got, two important things to know if it's omelette for lunch. However, by storing all your eggs in the same basket you're exposing yourself (and the eggs) to greater risk. If you were to drop that basket by accident … well, omelette would certainly be off the menu, and you'd have a hell of a mess to clean up. To add insult to injury, you'll also have the cost of replenishing the lost eggs.

But what about credit consolidation, that is, putting all of your lines of credit into the basket of a single lender, is that as risky as it is with eggs? The answer to that question hinges on a number of factors, which ought to be considered before making a decision. Of course, this is far easier said than done, for when the outcome of a decision has a considerable impact on our lives, the very thought of venturing on such a risky journey, irrespective of how beneficial it might be in the long run, often fills us with trepidation and foreboding. And this, in turn, can result in apathy and an unwillingness to take the necessary steps. So, in an attempt to make the process a little less painful, I present here the four main factors that must be considered before you decide to consolidate debt.

Factor 1: How many lines of credit are currently being serviced? If it is only a couple, then it might not be worth your while consolidating. Usually consolidation is a refuge for those poor souls who are prey to a veritable wolf pack of debt – that is, three snarling lenders and above. The decision ultimately hinges on Factor 2.

Factor 2: What is the interest rate of each line of credit and what is the total 'loan weight' value? I'll discuss this in more detail later.

Factor 3: Are you maintaining payment discipline? This is almost a contradiction in terms, for a person with multiple lines of credit running simultaneously clearly lacks monetary discipline. If you fit my stereotype – viz. you're drowning in debt and lack the discipline to keep your head above the water – consolidation may very well be for you. Read on.

Factor 4: Are you maintaining payment consistency? Have you set up direct debits or are you making payments on an ad hoc basis? Whereas Factor 3 is concerned with your intrinsic motivation to servicing your various lines of credit, Factor 4 asks you to consider how that debt is being serviced. What is your system? Do you even have a system? If you're currently wearing a bovine expression and your system is anything but a direct debit backed by brute discipline, get reading.

The factor of the highest importance here, and thus the one we must consider first, is **Factor 2: What is the interest rate of each line of credit and what is the total 'loan weight' value?** The primary purpose of credit consolidation is to reduce the interest rates of the various loans so that those usurious bastards – aka lenders – don't make off with as much of your hard-earned money. You with me? As illustrated by the story above of the young lady who got herself into a whole lot of store card debt, if you have multiple loans all on different interest rates, you could well be paying significantly more than you would if you consolidated them under a single lender. It is for this reason that you absolutely must take the time to calculate the combined interest rate or the per loan weight value. The most straightforward and accurate way to do this is by following the six-step process outlined below. But first, here's a list of items that might make calculating the per loan weight value easier:

- calculator (or abacus)
- pen
- paper
- strong black coffee
- a friend for moral support; or
- mobile phone with the Samaritans' helpline on speed dial

Got it all? Jolly good. Now get cracking.

Step 1

Make a list of your lines of credit, including the current remaining balance and interest rate. Regardless of what you do, consolidate or not, ensure you make *all* debt visible – do this today. I advise acquiring a whiteboard (sold in most stationery shops) and writing your debts in big letters on the board and placing it somewhere prominent so you can see it every day. I have one such board nailed to the wall beside my front door. If it doesn't feel like your debt is stalking you, then you're simply not doing it right. (For more ideas on this see **Tip 7: Make it *VISIBLE!*** in Tips, Tricks and Tools.) Okay, back to Step 1 – make a list of your credit lines. For example:

(a) On Tap: £1,000 @ 3.6%
(b) Gold Digger Loans: £1,000 @ 2.4%
(c) The Never-Never: £1,000 @ 4.1%

Step 2

Once you've made your list, however depressing it may be, you must now calculate the 'per loan weight value'. To achieve this, multiply each loan amount by its corresponding interest rate:

(a) £1,000 x 3.6% = £36
(b) £1,000 x 2.4% = £24
(c) £1,000 x 4.1% = £41

Step 3

Now add the individual per loan weight values together:
£36 + £24 + £41 = £101 (total loan weight value)

Step 4

Next, add the three loan amounts together to calculate the total loan amount:

£1,000 + £1,000 + £1,000 = £3,000 (total loan amount)

Step 5

(Nearly there!) Divide the total 'loan weight value' by total 'loan amount':

£101 ÷ £3,000 = 0.034

Step 6

Finally, multiply that figure by 100 to express it as a percentage:

0.034 x 100 = 3.4

That total loan weight value can be used to compare and contrast the various consolidation options available. With that value you can look for a lender offering consolidation services with a competitive interest rate – but preferably lower. And as long as there are no hidden fees or dubious contractual requirements, such as signing over your kids, a kidney or your house as collateral, then it makes perfect sense to consolidate.

The pros and cons of credit consolidation

Pros	Cons
You could reduce the overall interest rate, which will cut the cost of the loan considerably.	You could incur consolidation charges. You need to make sure you fully understand the terms and conditions of

It can ease the psychological and emotional burden that comes with worrying about multiple lines of credit. Even if the interest rate remained the same after consolidating, it might still be beneficial for your mental health to consolidate. You'll have to weigh this one up: is it worth jumping through a few bureaucratic hoops for the psychological relief of having only one loan to service as opposed to many?	consolidation before committing.
	Remember, any lender offering a consolidation service is doing so to make money off you. For that reason you must approach with caution. It is probably best to look at what the high-street banks are offering. Personally, I would not consider a consolidation service offered by small unfamiliar companies, however enticing their interest rate.
When servicing a single loan you can more readily see the debt shrink in size – which is serious psychological and motivational firepower. When servicing multiple loans, paying little bits here and there can, like running on a treadmill, feel as though you're getting nowhere, which is demoralising.	If it transpires that you could get a lower interest rate by consolidating, you must also consider the length of the term of the newly consolidated loan. For example, if the interest rate was lower by a couple of per cent but the fixed-term length was longer by a year or two, consolidating could actually be more costly.
It makes managing the debt simpler.	Consolidating could present a false picture of having

79

> reduced the debt size. 'Ah, wonderful, now that I've only one debt it wouldn't hurt to go take out another loan!'
>
> This sounds a bit far-fetched, but I've witnessed it in action – and to devastating effect.

A final thought on credit consolidation

Before reading on, I suggest you turn down the lights a little and pop on some soulful tunes such as Al Green's 'How Can You Mend a Broken Heart?' or Stevie Ray Vaughan's 'Riviera Paradise'.

Debt, like depression, disease and death, has become such a common feature of the human condition that we no longer perceive it as the pernicious evil that it truly is. It never used to be this way. Back when people used to pay for their wears and wants with money earned, debt was a rare and exotic entity few had ever encountered. Actually, for much of the nineteenth and twentieth centuries debt was abhorred. This was partly a consequence of the Protestant ethic.[3] The problem with this system and mindset, however noble and innocent it may sound to our sullied ears, is that it could never construct the immense economic wealth-producing machine that exists today. Something was done about that. Over many years our psychology was re-engineered. People were encouraged – more accurately,

---

[3] For a full and highly insightful analysis of the Protestant ethic and how it was slowly eroded, see Daniel Bell's brilliant *The Cultural Contradictions of Capitalism* (1996).

conditioned – to believe that ideals such as self-discipline, self-restraint and moderation were outdated, anachronistic and a sign of shameful simplicity.

The old world eventually crumbled under the inexorable march of modernity, and out of the wreckage a 'consumption society was emerging, with its emphasis on spending and material possessions' (Bell, 1996). But still, for 'consumption society' to really take off it needed an injection of high-octane fuel. At some point in the 1920s a bunch of American bankers realised that debt could just well be the fuel they were looking for. It was then that 'capitalism changed its nature ... by heavily encouraging the consumers to go into debt, and to live with debt as a way of life' (Bell, 1996). People today who are collectively saddled with more debt than any preceding generation in human history are the Frankensteinian creation of the consumption society.

The problem we now face is a psychological one: we must radically reform how we view debt. If you ever hope to be free from it, firstly you have to reject the belief that debt is merely 'a way of life'. It isn't, nor should it be, a way of life. As far as I am aware no other species subsists on a diet of debt. It is entirely a man-made creation and it has been created for the advantage of a few. For the rest, debt is an agony, a torment, a terrible burden that many people drag about until death do them part.

No doubt if you have persevered this far, you are among the ranks of the many and to your ankle is fettered a ball of debt; perhaps even multiple balls. Know this, whoever you are, not only do I sincerely sympathise with your plight, but I offer hope and reassurance that you can cut through the fetters and emancipate yourself from that most oppressive of masters. However, freedom comes at a cost. It requires discipline. It requires hard work. It requires a return to the ethic of our ancestors. You must, as of today, adopt 'the traditional value system, with its emphasis on thrift, frugality, self-control, and impulse renunciation' (Bell, 1996).

Though for many of us the prospect of returning to a simpler way of life seems bleaker than one of excessive consumption fuelled by a sickly diet of debt, if you value financial freedom above financial servitude you will make the necessary transition. You can do it!

Rule 7: Pay Yourself First

The premise of this rule is that before paying a bill or spending a single penny of your salary, the very first thing we should do is allocate a specific sum to our savings account. As sweeping statements go I think we're on safe ground to assert that the majority of people in the first week of receiving their monthly salary pay everyone else *but* themselves. Let me explain what I mean by this.

When our wages are deposited into our accounts at the start of each month, usually within the first minute or two, various companies suck some out; we call this paying our *bills*. Hot on the heels of paying our bills we might then pay our creditors; this is called paying our *debt(s)*. After paying our debt(s) we then fork out for the *necessities;* we call these *living costs* – food, toiletries, cosmetics, etc. Finally, when we've augmented the wealth of a host of faceless organisations and contributed to the wealth of an army of people we'll neither meet nor know, we treat ourselves; we call this staving off *suicidal depression*. But of all the people we pay, of all the people we make rich, the last person we pay, the last person we make rich, is ourselves.

This must stop!

I concede that much of what our wages go towards cannot be avoided. Given the choice, a hundred per cent of people would rather not pay their mortgage and instead deposit the money into a personal savings account. Also, we've got to eat – right? If the choice is between a roof over our heads and food on the table or satiating a savings account, the former is going to win out. And rightly so. To this line of reasoning I would be forced to capitulate. Yes, the gluttonous banks and building societies must receive their monthly libation, starvation must be kept at bay. However ...

However, it is still unacceptable not to be allocating a sum of your monthly earnings to a savings account. Saving money, in the opinion of most financial theorists, is *as* important (if not more so) as setting money aside for the mortgage, food and necessities. Really, we should regard our savings as we do any other mandatory bill and ensure to pay it promptly at the start of each and every month.

And there's one truly great difference with paying this bill as opposed to all the others: it's the only one that will ever make *you* rich (or at least provide you with a measure of financial security). When you pay that mortgage, depending on how far through your mortgage term you are, as much as 90% could be paying off interest and only 10% capital.[4]

I can remember receiving my very first annual mortgage statement. Back in those days, a little over ten years ago, companies used to post out paper copies of statements. I tore into the envelope with the expectancy of seeing a sizeable chunk chipped from the capital of my property. Instead I was greeted with a truly depressing figure. After faithfully paying my mortgage for a full year, which in total amounted to just over £6,500, I'd only shaved the paltry sum of £175 off the capital. I was truly distraught – not to mention disgusted. In fact such was my disgust that I rang the company. Once I'd beaten my way through a plethora of automated recordings I asked them where in god's good name did that £6,325 go. The unenthusiastic customer service person told me that the rest had gone on interest fees. Interest! But interest is a fiction. Banks don't even possess the tangible assets that they're 'lending' you; they've merely been granted governmental authority to issue loans. None of it is real! The only thing that is real is the time I spent earning that money. It was at this painfully naive point that the conversation concluded. But following that call I made a huge mistake. I did as the ostrich does and buried my head in the sand, continuing to pay that mortgage for ten more years before I finally took action. What an idiot!

---

[4] This explains why Robert Kiyosaki, author of *Rich Dad Poor Dad*, classifies home ownership as a liability, not, as is commonly believed, an asset. This is not the case for rental properties; Kiyosaki regards rental properties as assets as they pay an income against the capital investment. For more on Kiyosaki, see **Tip 10: Advance Your Knowledge**.

I apologise for that digression – it was sort of pertinent. Let's get this rule back on track, shall we?

So the idea of paying yourself first is to develop a healthy financial habit that taps into the power of compounding. The simplest way to understand compounding is to think of the snowball effect: a couple of insignificant snowflakes get together and, during their icy dance, attract more snowflakes which eventually sends them tumbling forward, in turn attracting more and more until, quite quickly, a snowball has formed that soon grows to a tremendous size.

When we save our money, although it may be in pitifully small amounts at the beginning, the total sum will steadily grow and, depending on the account that it is stashed in, attract interest which in turn will contribute to increasing its size. This is the process of compounding which Albert Einstein likened to one of the wonders of the world. 'He who understands it,' he purportedly said, 'earns it; he who doesn't, pays it.'

How do we get started with paying ourselves first?

Saving is one of those things we do to quieten our guilty conscience, like chucking a couple of pence into the cup of a street beggar, or running to the aid of an elderly person who's fallen when really all we want to do is laugh. Most people start the month with the good intention of saving (quietening the guilt), but then instantly make the pledge to save what they have leftover at the end of the month. For obvious reasons this is not a good strategy. From a financial perspective it is infinitely wiser to allocate a specific percentage of your net earnings to a savings account at the *start* of each month, not the end. This will sharpen your budgeting skills because you will be forced to be more careful with how much you spend during the coming month and on what you spend it (see **Rule 5: Create a Budget**).

When it comes to saving at the start of each month I would strongly advise against manual transactions – that is, going through the rigmarole of physically transferring funds. This is likely to result in three negative outcomes:

(1) You forget!
(2) Like Bilbo Baggins standing over the caldera, poised to drop the ring into the flames, you begin questioning whether you should allocate this month's savings.
(3) You decide to allocate slightly less this month because of X, Y, Z reasons.

One of the crucial keys to success here is to automate your savings contribution. Set up a direct debit to come out of your account on the 1st of every month. This way you will avoid a tussle with the demons of procrastination, and because the money will leave your account like any other bill you'll adjust your spending habits to accommodate the slight dip in available funds.

Before you set up your direct debit you will, of course, have to calculate exactly how much of your wage you can allocate to savings. This does require a bit of consideration. The amount you should save is analogous to the quandary Goldilocks found herself in when she serendipitously stumbled on three unattended bowls of porridge.

Too Hot! If the amount you decide to save is too much, you could find yourself struggling through the month. This may cause you to dip into your overdraft, which is something you must avoid at all costs. Or it may result in you siphoning funds back out of your savings. Breaking fiscal discipline is a slippery slope.

Too Cold! If the amount is too small, then you're not saving as much as you could be, which ultimately means that you'll fail to exploit the powers of compounding. Over the long haul – say, 5+ years – this could mean losses of thousands.

Just Right! I have put together an idea of how you might approach establishing the savings sum that is just right for you.

Let's say that at the end of each month you walk home with £1,200 in your back pocket, but before you reach the front door £600 has been sucked out of your wallet/purse to pay those pesky bills. In the blink of an eye your wage has halved, and the filching doesn't stop there. Not by a long chalk. Once you've set aside £150 for food and another £150 for living expenses you're left with £300 to play with. After a month of wearing your fingers to the bone, all you've got to show for it is 300 measly squid!

Remember **Rule 1: Spend Half, Save Half (aka the 50/50 maxim)**?

Right. So that £300 needs to be cut in twain, half of which will go to our savings account. Once a direct debit has been set up, for the first of every month, to transfer £150 out of your current account into a savings account, you can happily piss the remaining £150 up the wall of Primark if you want.

Saving can become an addiction – the more you do it, the more your savings increase, the more it makes you want to save. I heard about a man who'd become so addicted to saving that he constructed a makeshift washing line in his kitchen on which to peg used teabags so that he could dry them out and reuse them (if he had any intelligence, he would have just given up drinking tea). But the hardest part of any worthwhile endeavour is mustering the motivation to take the first step. Getting the ball rolling requires the most sweat, tears and toil, as Sisyphus can attest. But once you've got it going it gathers momentum quickly and before you know it, it delivers the same force as a wrecking ball.

So, with all that said, start saving today! Follow the four steps below and begin your journey to a better financial future.

> **Step 1)** Firstly you need to conduct a savings Q&A session. Ask yourself: am I currently saving a portion of my wage every month? If 'yes', before advancing to **Rule 8**, reconsider the Goldilocks Conundrum: are you saving enough? Could you be saving more? If you answered 'no' to the initial question, promptly proceed to the next step.
> **Step 2)** Calculate your outgoings and expenditure and determine how much you can allocate to a savings account. Do this right now.
> **Step 3)** Set up a direct debit immediately. To ensure saving allocation consistency it is imperative that you automate this process: establish a direct debit then, once you have factored this outgoing into your monthly budget, forget about it.
> **Step 4)** This is by far the hardest step as it demands that you maintain monetary discipline. Do not dip into your savings!

Rule 8: Form Good Financial Habits and Break the Bad Ones

Every single qualification for success is acquired through habit. Men [and women] form habits from futures. If you do not deliberately form good habits, then unconsciously you will form bad ones. You are the kind of man [or woman] you are because you have formed the habit of being that kind of man [or woman], and the only way you can change is through habit.

Albert E. N. Gray
The Common Denominator of Success (1940)

Before I talk about forming good financial habits, I would like to take this paragraph to sketch an outline of what constitutes a habit. The author of the opening quote places emphasis on how habits help us achieve success, but Mr Gray doesn't clarify what exactly they are – which leaves us scratching our heads. At its essence a habit is an action or process that we execute automatically and often – a simple everyday example would be that of brushing our teeth or completing our morning routine.

Depending on how they impact our lives – our health, psychology or socio-economic success – habits can be categorised as either good or bad. Bad habits are often as easy to identify as they are to form – smoking, drinking, gambling, pornography, takeaway food – but, as anyone who has formed one of the previous habits will readily attest, they are devilishly difficult to break. However, what you need to remember is that habits, unlike the Ten Commandments, are not set in stone. They can be formed and they can be broken. Also, they are precarious and fragile – the good ones, anyway – which is why when formed they must be protected, nurtured and regularly reinvigorated.

So what might 'habits' look like in a financial context?

To keep things simple (for my sake not yours), I've created a table laying out what constitutes good and bad financial habits. To encourage active participation, as any pedagogue worth his salt should, I want you to go get a pen (or better still, one of those radioactive bingo blotters) and tick (or daub) those habits that best describe your current financial practices in the table below.

Good financial habits	Bad financial habits
Paying yourself first – i.e. consistently saving a specified percentage of your wage at the start of every month.	Spending a substantial portion of your monthly earnings in the first week of the month. It is common practice among the financially undisciplined to enjoy a 'blowout' on payday.
Spending some time after you've been paid on allocating funds for necessary expenditure such as food, bills and expenses.	Failing to regularly review your accounts and finances for anomalous outgoings and unhealthy spending habits.
Rigidly sticking to your tight, clearly defined budget.	Carrying on a subscription to a service that you no longer use.
Concluding the month with leftover cash. Something, no matter how paltry, is infinitely better than nothing.	Paying more for services – loans, bills, subscriptions – than you need to.

Squirrelling away a little each payday into a second savings account for that treat or special something.	Treating yourself more than you should.
Maintaining strict fiscal discipline between pay cheques – i.e. resisting the temptation to buy things you don't need.	Digging a deeper hole of debt.
Dedicating a bit of time every quarter to reviewing your financial status and seeing where you could make a saving or reduce a bill/expenditure.	'Reviewing financial status? What's that?'
Using money you've earnt and not that fictitious stuff fabricated by a bank.	Spending on your credit card when you should be using earnings.
Being mindful to live well within your means.	Dipping into your overdraft.
Total good habits: ……	**Total bad habits:** ……

Take some time to tally up the good and the bad, making sure to jot the number in the totals box.

Hopefully the number you scribbled into the good habits box is greater than that in the bad habits box. If it isn't, do not fret. For habits, remember, are not set in stone: bad ones can be broken down and new, beneficial ones built in their place.

If you've an abundance of bad financial habits, then this gives you something to work on. Allow me to posit some advice here. Do not try to reform all of your bad habits at once. To try to change any more than one habit at a time is a recipe for failure. I suggest that you begin by compiling a list of bad habits and start with that habit you deem most pernicious. Once you've cracked it – and to do this may take a number of weeks, even months – then and only then should you move to the next habit on your hit list. What you might find is that the process of habit reformation gets easier as you go because you become more effective at breaking them.

Below is a list of habit-breaking Dos and Don'ts. You can adjust them to suit your personality and temperament.

Do define the habit clearly

At the outset, before taking up the sword and galloping off on your crusade to break a bad habit, you should state in simple terms exactly what it is and how you plan to reform it. I cannot overstate how important this is. In his book *Good Strategy/Bad Strategy*, Richard Rumelt tells us that 'the diagnosis for the situation should replace the overwhelming complexity of reality with a simpler story, a story that calls attention to its crucial aspects'.

Let's say that the bad habit you wish to reform is that of failing to review your account(s) at the start of each month (see **Rule 9: Regularly Review Your Finances**). After reading about the various financial ills that stem from accounting ignorance in that copy of *Penny-Pinchers* you've got stashed beside your toilet, you realise the risk you're running and resolve to change your behaviour. At this stage you're not sure what internal and/or external forces are pushing or pulling you away from dedicating a mere 10–20 minutes at the start of each month to reviewing your accounts but you know this is not a concern at the moment. Acknowledgement of the bad habit and a plan for how to break it are enough for now. Before putting your plan together and executing it you decide to define the bad habit in clear and simple terms. So, for example, you might state:

I am not consistently reviewing my accounts on an annual basis.

You may then want to outline why this habit is bad. You might find it useful to outline the potential calamitous outcomes. For example:

By not reviewing my account every month I run the risk of

- overspending
- running up debt
- failing to identify fraudulent activity
- failing to identify unhealthy spending habits

It's not until you have stated the bad habit clearly, being sure to associate it with its potential negative outcomes, that you begin the process of developing a strategy to make the necessary changes in behaviour.

(If you need to, reread the section in this book on Financial Strategy; better still, read Rumelt's book, *Good Strategy/Bad Strategy*.)

Don't try to reform any more than one habit at a time
I know I've already mentioned this one but it's important enough to merit repetition. To maximise your chances of breaking a bad financial habit we would be wise to focus only on one at a time. Every additional bad habit you tackle divides your powers of reform, thus weakening your resolve. Furthermore, you could inadvertently trigger a Jenga stack collapse: by failing in one habit you could cause a cascade of negativity, which will almost certainly spell disaster for those other habits you're trying to break. Were this to happen, and the probability increases the more habits you take on at any one time, you may well find yourself so demoralised by the whole enterprise that you beat a permanent retreat.

Do break down the process of habit reformation into manageable objectives/targets
When climbing the north face of the Eiger, Ranulph Fiennes said that he would look no further than his next hand-hold position, so about two or three feet ahead. By rigidly sticking to this strategy humanity's 'greatest living explorer' successfully summited the three thousand-metre mountain, seeing him complete a climb that is considered far more challenging than Mount Everest. By comparison habit reformation is the equivalent of tying your shoelaces. But even so, you stand a far greater chance of reaching your goal by focusing on one step at a time.

Don't be too hard on yourself
Yes, you do have to adopt a disciplined attitude and take on the role of the autocratic parent when enforcing behavioural change. However, you don't want to sprout a little black top-lip tache and

metamorphose into a Machiavellian tyrant. If you are too severe with yourself, you'll wind up feeling like crap. Habit reformation requires patience, persistence and, above all, compassion. When embarking on such a lofty personal endeavour as changing your behaviour – and we're the only species in the universe (that we know of) that can consciously run self-diagnostics and decide to 'reprogramme' itself – we must acknowledge our myriad flaws. Thus, if you do retrograde, remind yourself that this is part of the process and what matters is that you pick yourself up, dust yourself down and continue to persevere.

> To do something else means a change of habit ... And habits are the very dickens to change! Further, any change, even a change for the better, is always accompanied by drawbacks and discomforts.
>
> Arnold Bennett

Don't expect instant results

If you expect the bad habit to be banished within a few days, you'll likely succumb to despondency, apathy and perhaps an unwillingness to stay the course. Breaking long-established habits is notoriously challenging and can be a two-steps-forward, one-step-back process. It's like playing snakes and ladders: to ascend halfway up the board can take twenty plus rolls of the die yet it only takes one unlucky roll to send you sliding all the way back to the beginning again. Be prepared for this!

Do use positive reinforcement

In the psychological literature, of which there's a lot, research abounds supporting the idea that positive reinforcement is more effective at facilitating behavioural change than negative reinforcement. Put more succinctly, when it comes to breaking habits the carrot is far better than the stick. What might carrot reinforcement look like though? Well, sincerely praising yourself when you reach a certain milestone would constitute a method of positive reinforcement. Other examples include rewards, treats and/or celebrations – yes, *celebrations*. Let's say that the bad habit you desire to break is that of dipping into your overdraft. You know that to stand any chance of succeeding you must tie your purse strings in knots and stick to a budget that's tighter than a duck's squirter. And for thirty agonisingly long days you are going to observe a spending fast and deny yourself all those hedonistic luxuries to which you have become addictively accustomed. What you could do as a means of positively reinforcing this behaviour-change strategy is to say that you will treat yourself with half of whatever you have left in your account at the end of the month.

Rule 9: Regularly Review Your Finances

The state of a person's fiscal affairs could, I think, be accurately predicted depending on how they answer the following question: do you regularly review your finances? If that person answers in the affirmative, then I would confidently wager one whole jelly bean (aka a day's pay) that they enjoy relatively sound financial health. If the answer comes in the form of a scratch of the head and another question ('duh … regularly what?'), then I would confidently stake a similar wager that that person is wallowing in one of four muddy financial quagmires:

(1) Debt. People who lack the fiscal discipline required to check their accounts on a consistent basis are more than likely

to be drowning in a cesspit of debt. Why? Because they're bereft of monetary discipline, and because they're probably afflicted with a laissez-faire attitude toward personal finances, both potentially dangerous qualities at a time when credit, loans and finance are so freely doled out. There hasn't been an age when debt was so easy and cheap to acquire.

(2) In their overdraft. A person who fails to regularly review their accounts and monitor the ebb and flow of their financial currents will inevitably write a promissory note to the bank at some point before their next pay cheque arrives in the post. And on the slippery slope they have stepped!

(3) Wasting what precious little they have by paying over the odds for household bills.

(4) Poor. People who tend not to have a pot to piss in, and there are legions of these piss-pot-less people, in all probability got to be this way precisely because they do not actively review and scrutinise their finances. And if it isn't directly responsible for making them poor, accounting ignorance is certainly compounding the problem.

I've often wondered why people willingly wallow in financial swamps. Why, I've asked myself with some perplexity, do they tolerate that lamentable condition? Why don't they pull themselves out of the quagmire in which they are sinking? Why don't they at least try? I have, in my search for answers, happened upon two possible explanations. The first (drawn from my own experience) arises from the fact that few of us are ever taught what Robert Kiyosaki calls 'financial literacy'. On the back pages of his book *Rich Dad Poor Dad*, Kiyosaki tells us that 'the main reason people struggle financially is because they have spent years in school but learned nothing about money. The result is that people learn to work for money ... but never learn to have money work for them.' I agree with Kiyosaki's central contention – viz. too few people are adequately inducted into the world of financial management. However, I find myself dissenting at the point where he casts an incriminating finger at schools for the dearth in financial literacy. (Schools, more accurately *teachers* and support staff, fulfil an imperative and indispensable social function that far exceeds inculcating the next generation; for many vulnerable students, and there are a disconcerting number of young people who fall into that category, schools provide a vital support network.)

The job of teaching young people how to count their pennies should fall to parents, not schools and certainly not financial institutions. I'd quite like to know how many parents actually take the time to sit down with their progeny and give them a lesson about money. When I was young I can clearly recall my mum encouraging me to open a savings account. Back then the banks gave you a little book, rather like a passport, in which deposited or withdrawn funds were documented. I used to love seeing my money mount up as I squirrelled away any cash I'd managed to scrimp, save and/or steal. But not once did Mother ever sit me down and try to impart a modicum of financial acumen. The tuppence of financial knowledge I did acquire came into my possession only as a consequence of growing up in a household where one parent possessed a few healthy financial habits: an abhorrence of debt, a propensity to diligently save a sizeable slice of earnings, and a near unhealthy obsession with budgeting – in short, Mother was a closet Mervyn King and kept a watertight fiscal ship. Beyond this parsimonious formative financial education I've since had to spend considerable time teaching myself through the only two alternative channels available – reading and experience (aka making mistakes).

So other than sheer ignorance, what other reason could account for why so many people are oblivious to their financial comings and goings? Personally, I think apathy is complicit in this crime. Yes, it is my humble contention that many people quite simply couldn't give a shit about their financial state of affairs. What wheel has come loose to cause this psychological derailment from the financial tracks? Everyone will have their own reasons for this. However, if this attitude persists (or worse, degenerates into nihilism), then the apathetic person, the person who is bereft of the modicum of discipline required to regularly review their finances, will forever founder on the financial rocks.

Of all the rules, this one is by far the easiest – and what's more it gets easier still if/when you get your accounts in order. I think you'll agree that when a room is kept clean and tidy it requires much less maintenance than one that has been allowed to degenerate into a pigsty. Not only does the tidy room consume fewer calories to keep clean but it doesn't incite the same fear and foreboding when it comes to that time of the week when you pull on a pair of pink rubber gloves, tie on the pinny and break out the polish. Maintaining our finances is directly analogous. By setting aside a mere 5 to 10 minutes at the start, middle and end of each month to review your finances you stand a much greater chance of avoiding debt, dipping into your overdraft, wasting money on household bills, and being poor. For such a small investment in time you stand to make substantial return. And with the advent of the internet and mobile phone banking the process has been rendered almost effortless.

When and how to review your finances

Before we establish the *how* we must firstly determine the *when*. I submit that you should set aside some time at the end of each week to review your finances. That way you will be able to accurately gauge if you are staying within pre-specified budgets, hitting reduced expenditure targets, and, most importantly, it allows you to identify anomalous outgoings – that is, fraudulent activity. Not to put the scarers on you but more accounts are hacked and infiltrated today than ever before. It has been estimated that around a million people every year are victims of banking fraud, which collectively costs the financial system in excess of £300 million.[5] The move to a technological banking system, where we can freely access our accounts via the internet and make transactions at the speed of light has its positives, but it also has many negatives. By regularly reviewing our finances we stand a much greater chance of identifying fraudulent activity early on. This in turn enables us to put a stop to it before we've been done out of a princely sum.

The preferred method of defrauding accounts closely resembles how a tick sustains its existence. Allow me to explain. If on the first transaction the parasite withdrew a sizeable sum from its host's account, they would almost certainly attract unwanted attention from either the bank or account holder. This would instantly put a stop to any future transactions. The tick gets burnt off the back of the dog's neck. (And good riddance, you little

---

[5] *Watchdog* blog, 'Bank Fraud: Easy to be a victim – hard to get your money back?' 8 April 2020, *BBC*.
https://www.bbc.co.uk/programmes/articles/1KD4OdVsOFmtnRv4ByszLr8/bank-fraud-easy-to-be-a-victim-hard-to-get-your-money-back. Last accessed: 17 November 2020.

bastard!) However, the tick, in an effort to ensure its own survival, has developed a safer method of feeding off its host without drawing unwanted attention. Sums of money are withdrawn in small, insignificant amounts arbitrarily throughout the month – £3.24 here, £5.57 there. These are the size of spends that typically get swallowed by the sound of so many monthly transactions. I don't know the average number of monthly transactions made by the average person, but I bet it's north of 20 (not including fixed bills and direct debits). With so much financial traffic taking place, a couple of small sums are likely to go unnoticed unless the account is regularly monitored.

Placing parasites and fraudulent activity to one side for a moment, if you cultivate the habit of reviewing your finances on a weekly basis, you will be able to track fiscal progress and adjust spending accordingly. Say, for example, that after all your necessary outgoings have been sucked out of your account by a different species of parasite (banks, utilities, the taxman) you are left with £500 to last until next payday, and of late you've got into the awful habit of draining your account almost dry. With a week to go until the next pay cheque you're just a drop or two away from dipping into your overdraft. In a moment of sobriety you resolve – really resolve this time – to exercise a modicum of monetary maturity and limit yourself to £100 spending cash each week (aka establishing a fixed budget). This way you will have £100 left in your account at the end of the month and if you stay strong and maintain this healthy habit for a year you'll have saved over £1,000.

Realistically the only way you are going to achieve this objective is by keeping a close track of your spending and by reviewing your finances on a weekly basis. If you set the above goal and only bother to check your account on payday, the chances of success are slim at best. To stand any hope of staying within that £100 budget you're going to have to run a tight ship, which will require a conscientious captain at the financial helm.

Earlier I said that reviewing your finances was dead easy and that if your accounts are in order it shouldn't take any more than five minutes a week. To substantiate this claim, because I don't want anyone thinking I trade in falsehoods, I have included below an example account statement. Together we will review the statement of financial transactions and form a summative opinion of our review.

Before we begin, allow me to impart a few words of advice on this process. When parsing a statement I find it best to proceed from the most recent transaction through to the oldest – which should be the beginning of whatever week you're on. So we work backwards chronologically. As you progress down the list of transactions your primary concern is to ensure that all outgoings are kosher and that there are no anomalous withdrawals. Once you've swept your account for ticks the process is repeated a second time but now you're looking out for unhealthy spending trends.

Example account statement

Date	Description	Type	In (£)	Out (£)	Balance (£)
04 Apr 2020	STARCUPS COFFEE	DEB		13.50	2,035.50
04 Apr 2020	VANITY WEAR	DEB		120.00	2,049.00

03 Apr 2020	STARCUPS COFFEE	DEB		11.10	2,169.00
03 Apr 2020	POUND STRETCHER	DEB		1.00	2,180.10
03 Apr 2020	JOE'S PIZZA	DEB		18.50	2,181.10
02 Apr 2020	STARCUPS COFFEE	DEB		12.20	2,199.60
02 Apr 2020	CREDIT CARD PAYMENT	DEB		300.00	2,211.80
02 Apr 2020	CAR INSURANCE	DD		25.00	2,511.80
02 Apr 2020	NETFLIX	FPI		10.00	2,536.80
02 Apr 2020	CREDIT INTEREST	INT	2.61		2,546.80
01 Apr 2020	STARCUPS COFFEE	DEB		10.00	2,544.19
01 Apr 2020	WATER RATES	DD		25.95	2,554.19
31 Mar 2020	UNION CONTRIBUTION	DD		17.96	2,580.14
31 Mar 2020	WAGE	DC	1,636.00		2,598.10

In performing this exercise we are limited by the fact that the statement is fictitious, which of course means that we do not know if any of the transactions are anomalous. However, we can still get a feel for the process of reviewing an account statement while sharpening our eye so as to better spot unhealthy spending habits.

If I were to ask you to circle the transactions that you think constitute excessive spending, which ones would you paint a bullseye around? I agree, that £120 at Vanity Wear was a touch decadent. But let's say you can justify it, that you genuinely needed to replace your business costume, are there any other transactions you would circle? Correct! Starcups Coffee should definitely get dragged in front of the firing squad. No one needs to visit a coffee shop four times in as many days. Yet you'd be surprised how many people do. And just look at the cost of all that coffee – £46.80! That's in one week! If that habit were allowed to persist, this account would see nearly £200 frittered away in a month on fattening coffee-flavoured milk drinks and ultra-processed confectioneries. But now our attention has been drawn to this unhealthy spending habit we can look to stamp it out – or at least flatten it. When we come to review our account the following week we should see an absence or steep decline in the number of payments made to Starcups Coffee.

Maybe the best way to conclude **Rule 9** is by insisting that, as of this very second, you carefully place this book to one side, open your account (assuming that you're not a Luddite and have set up internet/mobile phone banking), and put into practice the principles we've covered and start reviewing your finances today! Irrespective of where you are in the week go do this now.

Done? You better had! Okay, here's a quick recap of **Rule 9**:

- Cultivate the habit of regularly reviewing your accounts.
- Review your accounts either at the start or at the end of each week (once a month or once a year is not frequent enough).
- The two main reasons we review our accounts is (a) to ensure that no fraudulent transactions are being made

and (b) to keep an eye on our spending habits to ensure we are sticking to our budget:
- o on your **first sweep** of your statement, aim to identify any anomalous transactions.
- o on your **second sweep,** look out for unhealthy spending trends and make sure you're on target with your budget.

Rule 10: Live Within Your Means

Oscar Wilde once said 'Anyone who lives within their means suffers from a lack of imagination.' What a wit old Wilde was, truly one of a kind. Personally I'm not so sure about the accuracy of his statement. It seems a bit open and closed to me. If you choose to live within your means, for whatever reason, you are bereft of imagination?

What I like about generalised sweeping statements is that they're so easy to break; when tested under the slightest weight of reason they snap like pieces of IKEA furniture. I think one would be hard-pushed, even if they had Wilde's immense intelligence, to maintain a convincing argument that Socrates, Plato and Aristotle, for example, lacked imagination. 'Is this going anywhere?' you may ask. Well, yes, actually it is. These three Greek philosophers made an incalculable contribution to the collective intelligence of our species. They certainly didn't lack imagination. Yet even though their teachings and theories differ in many ways, they share one characteristic: they all espoused simple living. Socrates walked about Athens barefooted and wore the same soiled toga (which came to be called Socrates' second skin); he also shunned all material possessions. Plato was offered the chance of wealth, riches and social prestige but turned them down for a life of learning and simplicity. Aristotle is the father of the all-things-in-moderation doctrine. A significant portion of his *Nicomachean Ethics* – the first and last treatise on right living – is given over to discussing the dangers of departing from moderation. He warns us that the person

> who pursues the excess of things pleasant, or pursues to excess necessary objects, and does so by choice, for their own sake and not at all for the sake of any result distinct from them, is self-indulgent [and indulgence invariably leads to the sorry dilapidation of the self].

To practice living within your means – and implementing it as a lifelong practice – does not mean that you lack imagination. And if you do decide to adopt this lifestyle, you'll not only find yourself in the company of a handful of humanity's greatest thinkers, but you'll also reap the many rewards and benefits on offer. It is to those benefits that we shall now turn our attention.

Of all the benefits available to the person who is prepared to begin living within their means, the near impossibility of getting into debt is, for me, the lowest hanging fruit. Thus I shall pick it and with it, launch into my exposition. Extenuating and unlikely circumstances aside (e.g. you've been screwing the taxman out of his dividend for the past twenty years and he's just found out) you simply cannot run into debt if you live within the sphere of your earnings, however bounded or constricted that sphere may be. It's only when you step out of your financial sphere into the badlands of lavish living that you might find yourself falling in with horrible old Debt and his evil band of bad appetites. Such miserable company can be avoided if you are sensible and strong-willed enough to spend less than you earn, to delay gratification and say no to wants and desires (see **Rule 4: Delay Gratification**).

Learning to live on little more than what is necessary is a stoic virtue. Seneca and his philosophical forebears propounded the importance of exercising moderation for the bounties it confers, such as a sharpened sense of what matters in life. A Dionysian lifestyle will not bring about happiness,[6] but it may well bring about financial ruination, the degradation of the soul (if you believe in such a thing) and the degeneration of personal health, and contribute to the demise of the planet. Who would have thought that so much rides on so simple a concept?

The Stoics also maintained that it was in the fires of moderate living that we can best temper the mettle of self-discipline. By being able to say to one's urges and desires, 'No, I have enough, thank you', we can learn to cultivate and grow an invaluable quality – and one which few will ever possess. Just take a look around at the state of your fellow humans; see how many are mired up to their eyeballs in debt, are grossly overweight and suffering terribly from man-made diseases that manifest in the presence of excess.

Living within our means doesn't have to be limited to cutting back on expenditures. It can encompass an entire reformation of one's lifestyle – if you want it to, of course.

---

[6] Dionysus was the Olympian god of good living, of pleasure, festivity but also madness and wild frenzy.

Learning to live within your means or below it is to liberate yourself from the shackles of material want. Many millions of people are 'living' from one want to the next. I know people who truly believe life is not worth the bother if they cannot see looming large on the horizon a holiday or new thing. To these sad souls, daily existence is a drab grey canvas without the colour of perpetual consumerism.

Another positive impact that living within our means can confer is to bequeath us with more time. In the many personal accounts I have read where people have shared their experiences of adopting a simple lifestyle, a surfeit of free time is a frequently reported benefit. These 'simple livers' claim that by stepping out of the consumer rat race, they were wasting less time chasing after consumables and consequently had more time at their disposal. Many of those simple living testimonials described how they directed this new-found time to rehabilitating an atrophied talent, or augmenting their stock of knowledge, or learning a new skill such as speaking a foreign language or playing a musical instrument.

It never ceases to amaze me the staggering abundance of benefits a seemingly simple lifestyle change can bring. Who could have imagined that by living within our means we could forge durable self-discipline? That we could free up more time? And to think that these benefits, and others, are just waiting patiently to be had! Some of them could be yours today.

So let's focus on what living within your means looks like, because I certainly don't want to paint the 'simple liver' in the sullen and sorry image cast by that most doleful of protagonists

Brand, the ultra-aesthetic priest of Ibsen's profound imagination. Personally, if the choice were between living the austere life of Brand or one of decadent excess modelled by Mr Micawber (from Dickens's *David Copperfield*), I'd choose the latter in the blink of an eye even if it did mean debtors prison and exile to Australia. Actually on second thought ...

> Or perhaps you win if you have the most toys or the best toys. And if you play the game right, you can buy each toy now if the down payment and the monthly payments are low enough. Well, if you follow that rule, you'll be led down the path of financial slavery as you acquire more and more consumer debt.
>
> Van K. Tharp

Living within your means doesn't imply that you have to adopt a post-apocalyptic lifestyle, degenerate into a quasi-hunter-gather and go on daily foraging jaunts to the local park. It also doesn't mean annexing yourself from civilisation and spurning the many boons modern society has to offer – such as running water, central heating, electricity and an abundance of calories. Nor do you have to punish yourself by enforcing perennial deprivation. At its bare minimum living within your means requires only that you do not spend more than you earn – that you never exceed your income. This doesn't prohibit you, if you really wish to live a lavish lifestyle, from expanding your income so that you may acquire more stuff. If that's where you're at, go beg your boss for a few more shifts or start applying for a second job. Alternatively, instead of wasting your life working to consume, you could strive to find fulfilment in frugality. It's really a very pleasant place once you break through the crusty chrysalis of Western indoctrination.

You're not a failure if you live in a modest-sized house and drive a Skoda, or cycle.

You're not a failure if you have an anorexic wardrobe.

You're not a failure if you don't possess the latest technological thing.

You're not a failure if you make do with what you've got.

And finally, a cheap coat does not make you cheap![7]

On the contrary, the Western interpretation of what constitutes as success is in many ways more closely aligned to the symptoms of a mental sickness (of the sort described in Louis Sass' immense *Madness and Modernism*). And the truth is, it's all very much the opposite to the prevailing zeitgeist. That is, the person who self-actualises through material possessions, who attempts to imbue 'success' by cladding themselves in a garb of conspicuous consumables, is not showcasing success but advertising their prepubescent psychology, emotional instability and rampant

---

[7] In his exploratory exposition on why people willingly – even eagerly! – pay over the odds for commodities and consumables, Thorstein Veblen, coiner of the concept of conspicuous consumerism, cites a sage who summed up this psychological affliction in the terse dictum: 'A cheap coat makes a cheap man' and who wants to be seen as cheap? (*The Theory of the Leisure Class* – p. 95.) The point, of course, is that it's pure poppycock propagated by corporations – material belongings do not maketh the man or woman.

insecurity. (Not to mention their complete inability to distinguish that which possesses genuine value.) Truly, the prick-pipe puffing prat condomed in a Canada Goose jacket popping the kids to school in the gas-guzzling Land Rover Vogue while nonchalantly thumb swiping their iPhone is screaming three things: 1) I give not a single shit about urban pollution (I'm happy to toxify the very air that I and my progeny breathes); 2) I have absolutely no idea how to adequately allocate superfluous income; 3) this is the only way I can feel superior to other members of my species.

* * *

I opened this rule with a quote from the celebrated writer and poet Oscar Wilde in which he claimed that those who live within their means lack imagination. I have endeavoured to demonstrate that precisely the opposite is the case and that not only is there no correlative link between living within your means and an absence of imagination, but also that some of the most brilliant and creative thinkers were staunch advocates of practising moderation. If all this has failed to stir your interest in living within your means and you still harbour a sceptical opinion of the concept, then it is now time for me to play my trump card. I will conclude with some more of Wilde's words.

While wallowing pitifully in abject penury in a dingy Parisian hotel, Wild wrote a letter of desperation to his publisher. In it the man who had earlier mocked 'simple livers' had this to say:

> 'This poverty really breaks one's heart: it is sale [filthy], so utterly depressing, so hopeless. Pray do what you can [to wit send me some money!] ...'

Examples of Financial Idiocy: An Interlude

Having read through the ten Penny-Pincher rules, I imagine the reader is feeling somewhat fatigued from clambering up and over the many craggy constrictions that are to be implemented if one wishes to ascend the summit of sound financial health. For the person who has experienced little to no monetary discipline thus far in their lives they may well be reeling in shock from the strict and seemingly severe regime laid out. Your financially unfit mind may have struggled the way an obese person struggles at one of those military-style fat-fighter camps. So, because some of you will have worked hard to get this far and may even have started to implement some of the rules, I thought that as a treat we could enjoy a brief interlude and take a look at some examples of financial idiocy.

In each example I've encapsulated the characteristics of that particular form of financial idiocy – the behaviours you'll likely see exhibited by that archetype. Then I provide an anecdotal incident of the financial idiot in action.

The reader could well ask what the purpose of this exercise is. Well, we humans like nothing more than to revel in the misfortunes of other people. I know I do. So why not enjoy a little pick-me-up at another person's expense. However, the main purpose of this exercise is to educate. One of the best ways to learn is through observing the mistakes made by others. You'll have read elsewhere in this book: the intelligent person learns from their own mistakes whereas the philosopher learns from the mistakes of others. Well, if this maxim has any merit, wouldn't it be wise to take a more philosophical approach to our finances?

Gotta Have the Next Best Thing!

Financial freedom is really a new way to think about money. Most people think they win the money game by having the most money and the most toys. This rule has been set up by other people to mislead you. If you follow it, someone else besides you will win the money game.

Van K. Tharp
Trade Your Way to Financial Freedom

This is the person who's never satisfied with the thing they've got and are always on the lookout for something better. Usually they focus on a particular commodity, such as technology and computing, clothing, or gadgets. When they acquire the latest and best thing they soar in the sunshine for a while on the thermals of the buyer's high. But this updraft of euphoria soon wears off and they begin falling to earth at a rapid rate of knots like a punctured hot-air balloon. It's at this point that the novelty of the thing has worn off, the fine lacquered lustre having lost its dazzling hue, and they start to look for the next new best thing. This ridiculous circulatory process, which I was once caught in, will continue unabated unless:

(a) the person is suddenly and unexpectedly struck down by an epiphany and realises the stupidity of their behaviour;
(b) they die.

A close relative of mine perfectly exemplifies this archetype. His consumer item of choice was high-grade stereo equipment. At first (many moons ago), he purchased a relatively expensive stereo that he was satisfied with for a long time. But at some point he succumbed to next-best-thing delusion and ever since has sought to acquire the best stereo system under the stars. From the one-piece stereo (an inferior audio contraption that only ignorant brutes or people hard of hearing would play music through), he moved on to 'separates' (the equivalent of tossing aside your spliff to take up the syringe). No doubt about it, a stereo system comprised separates does produce a noticeably higher-quality auditory experience. However, it comes at a substantial cost and, as any seasoned audiophile well knows, when you upgrade one component of your system, all the other major components have to be upgraded in tandem.

I once asked this relative how much he had spent on stereo equipment over the years. He flashed me a wry smile (audiophiles, as with anyone afflicted with this species of financial idiocy, love to be asked how much their stuff costs) and set about performing the strenuous calculations required to arrive at a reasonably accurate approximation of all the money wasted. After five long minutes of 'The Cyrus series 8 cost two grand ... But then I upgraded to the Naim Nova which cost four grand ... And the Cambridge Audios cost ...', he arrived at a palpitation-inducing estimate of £38,000! The reader may well raise an incredulous eyebrow at this figure. But I can confirm, having intermittently seen his system evolve over the years, that his estimation was probably only a thousand or two off the mark.

Crazy right? What's crazier still is that this extreme example isn't as rare as you might think. I've known people spend incalculable thousands on watches, cars, clothes, all chasing the unobtainable next best thing. The only winner in this misguided game is the capitalist, the corporation, the fat cat. The consumer loses at every stage in the hunt for the elusive white whale:

- No doubt the consumer is selling their own labour at a discounted rate. Thus they are out of pocket before they've even dipped their hand into it.
- The thing purchased is always priced above what it's really worth. How else can the fat cat make a profit?` (Marx exposed this in *Capital Volume 1*: the capitalist augments their coffers by, amongst other techniques, underpaying the employee and overcharging the consumer.)
- Usually the person seeking the next best thing sells the redundant thing to finance the new acquisition. Consequently, they incur yet another loss by selling the second-hand thing for much less than it's worth. (Because who wants to pay a fair price for second-hand stuff when credit is so cheap?)
- They make another loss each time they buy the next best thing because, like the previous best thing, it is priced high so that fat cat can keep himself in caviar.

I was once caught in the trap of this form of financial idiocy myself. My next best thing of choice was guitars. I'd buy a guitar after convincing myself that it was the best plank of wood with six strings since bread was sliced, and I'd play it for a year or so. Then the lustre would wear off (or I'd spot a new best guitar) and I'd begin the process of convincing myself that I really ought to trade in my rubbish old guitar for a spanking new one; after all, I'm never going to be Stevie Ray Vaughan with a battered old woodworm-riddled guitar.

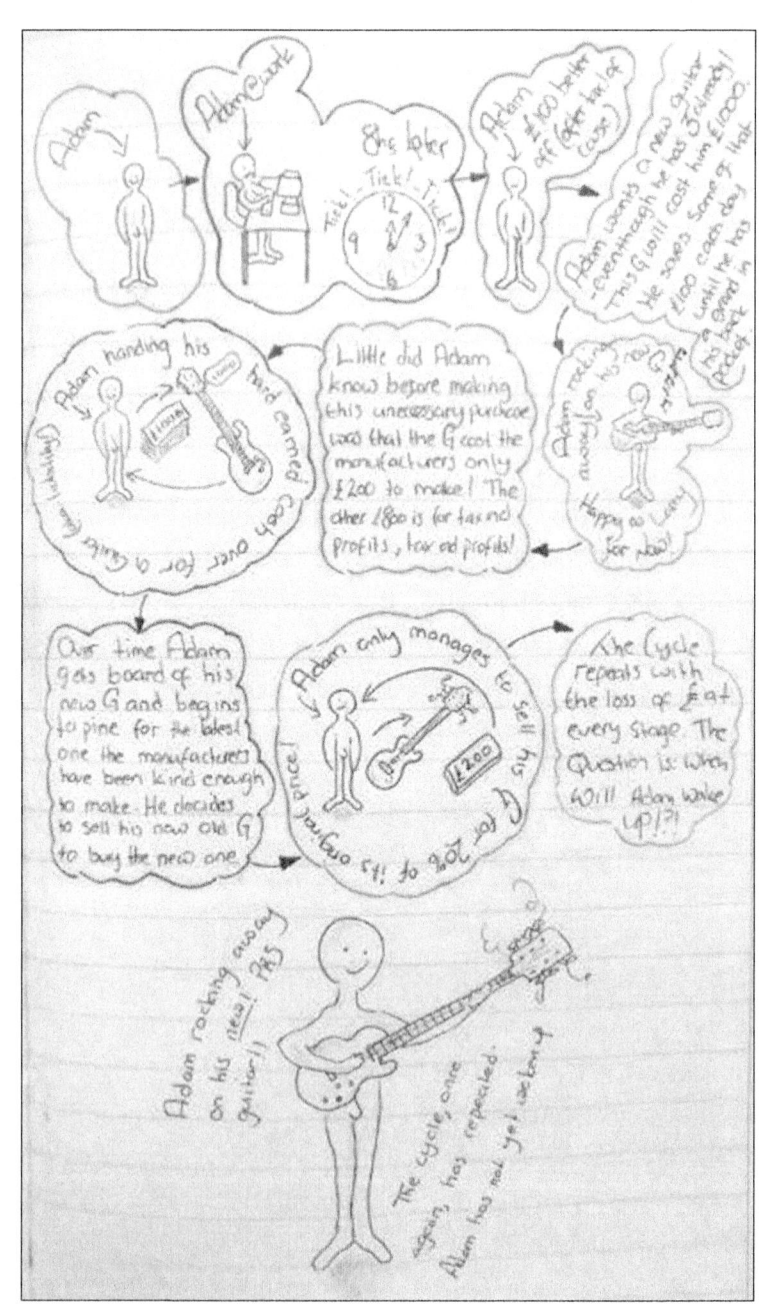

Banksy, watch out!

Okay, so you've enjoyed a little laugh at this idiot's expense. Well, now I invite you to complete your own comic book sketch – that is, if you fit the bill of the 'next best' idiot.

Below you'll find a collection of boxes. In the first box identify your consumer item of choice – it could be a pushbike, a car, watches, computers; whatever thing you keep chasing. Then proceed to create the cycle, making sure to include how much money is being lost at each stage. At the end of the cycle calculate how much money has been wasted. If you dare, try to recall the number of times you have been through the cycle of chasing the next best thing. The example above is just one cycle. Before I woke up to my idiocy I had completed ten laps to the tune of about £12,000.

(If you're not quite the talented artist that I clearly am, you can forgo the illustrations.)

Start here:

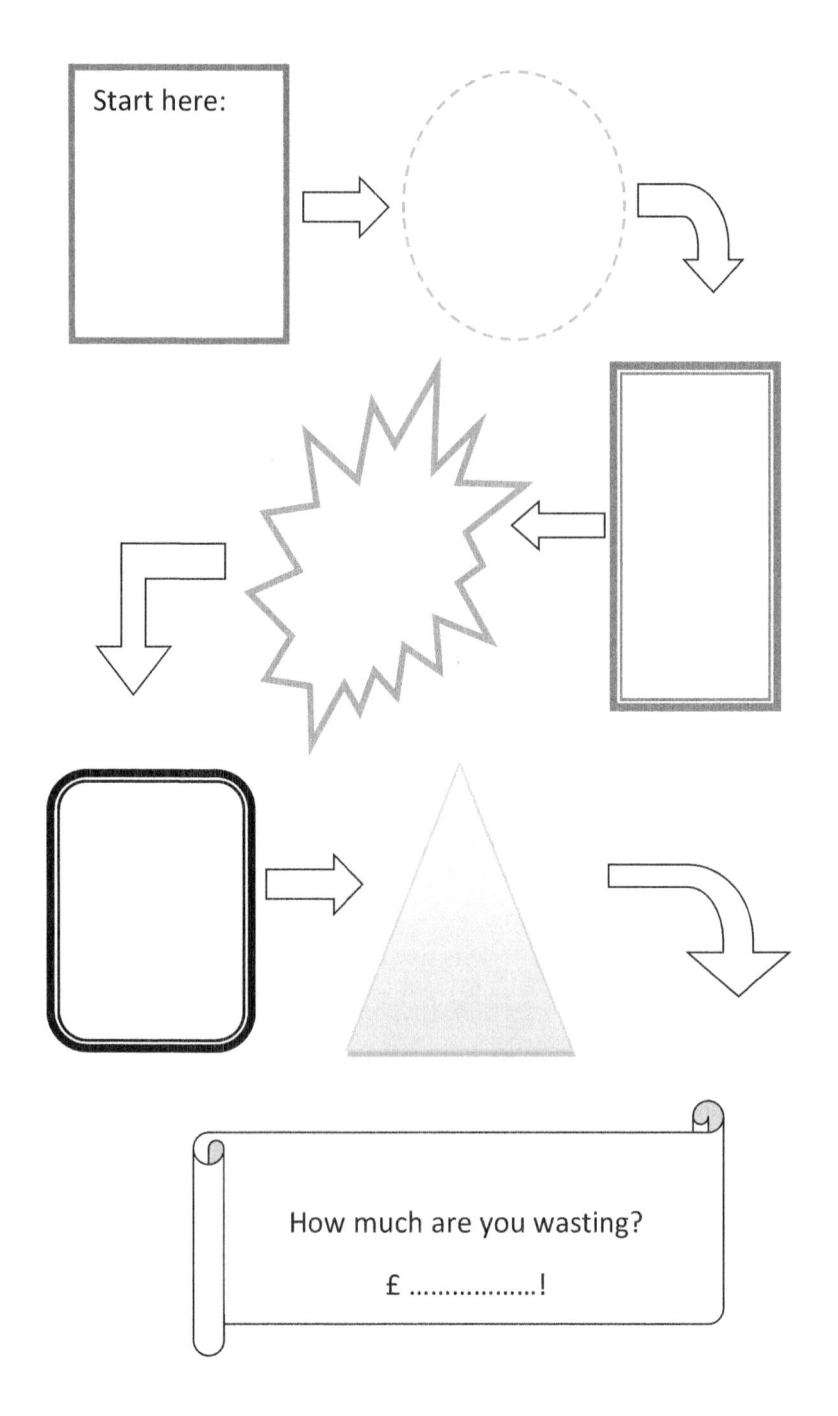

How much are you wasting?

£ ....!

Playing Financial Dodgems

This is where we watch people crashing and smashing from one bad financial decision to another. They have no idea where they're going or what they're doing but one thing's for sure, they'll waste a shit-ton of dough while they're at it.

I once worked with a guy who was an inveterate financial dodgems driver. He bought a motorbike for £8,000 and a year or two later, when he realised riding motorbikes was like playing Russian roulette and is absolutely no fun in the winter, he sold it for a third of the original price. When his car started to show signs of age, he traded it in for a fancy off-roader that cost £15,000. Shortly after that decadent splurge he bought his wife a sports car for £25,000 (a marriage-saver, as he called it). About two years later he was toying with the idea of selling the off-roader to buy one of those fashionable camper vans. I asked him how much a fashionable camper van goes for these days. Apparently you wouldn't get much change out of £40,000!

Now I know it could be argued that if he wants to waste his money on expensive and wholly unnecessary modes of transport, that is his prerogative. And I agree: a mature adult is entitled to spend their income as they choose. However, I still cannot help question the irresponsible and reckless allocation of money. Call me old-fashioned but if a parent decides to waste money on 'toys' when they could provide their progeny with financial assistance, I call that person an idiot. That £48,000 (possibly £88,000) would have given his two teenage kids a hefty hoist up the property ladder or served as nice nest egg for when they reached an age of maturity. Instead it's gone into the pocket of a slimy used-car salesman.

Perpetually Pissing it up the Wall

These people tend to waste their money on ... well, everything and anything. They're not, as is often erroneously assumed, confined to a single demographic – that is, the poor – but can be seen in all levels of society from the low-paid to the financial upper crust. Thus the person who perpetually pisses it up the wall can earn a decent wage and bring home the bacon, yet still have little to no money in savings, find themselves in their overdraft at the end of each month and, because of all their superfluous spending, have next to nothing to show for it. They are like financial black holes – when money comes into their possession, irrespective of the quantities, it instantly vanishes without trace.

If you're not the kind of person who perpetually pisses their money up the wall, you've probably met someone who fits the bill. Back in my Royal Marine days I came into contact with many such archetypes. But the sore thumb who stands out from the pack of financial misfits was a friend of mine called Pete. He was a top lad, salt-of-the-earth type who didn't have a care in the world, lived from one day to the next and never had a single penny in his pocket for the three years that we worked together. I remember once he disclosed how much debt he was in. He told me, with perfect sangfroid, that he was nine grand in the red. After shaking off the shock I sought to cure my incredulity by clarifying how many zeros followed that nine. It was three – £9,000.

But I still found it difficult to believe that Pete could be in so much debt. Here's why. He didn't own a car; he didn't have any 'dependants' (aka kids) and he lived on barracks, which meant that his living expenses were extremely low (at the time, accommodation and food deductions amounted to a measly £125 a month). So after the Ministry of Defence took a small slice of Pete's pie, he'd still be left with a sizeable chunk – perhaps as much as £1,500. So I had to ask, how was he in so much debt? 'Fuck knows,' he replied, 'but I am.'

Coarse and candid though his answer was, it perfectly sums up the attitude of person who pisses their money up the wall. They earn, they spend and they're completely clueless as to where it goes. I probed Pete for an insight into what exactly he spent his money on, but he couldn't readily answer that question either, settling for vague and ambiguous excuses such as 'Well I like to live it up a bit' and 'I enjoy a good holiday.' I could tell, by his uncharacteristic reticence, that he preferred not to talk about his dire financial state of affairs. Later on I asked a mutual friend if he knew of Pete's pecuniary plight. He did. I asked if he knew the cause. He said that Pete frittered his money – and anyone else's, for that matter – on alcohol, cigarettes, meals out, lavish holidays and prostitutes – oh, and he was currently developing a gambling addiction. 'Wow,' I remember thinking, 'he's nearly got a full house of vices. All he needs now is to get himself hooked on a class A drug.'

Pete is the personification of the person who perpetually pisses their money up the wall.

The tell-tale signs of this archetype include a mixture of the following:

- always short on money;
- in debt;

- frequently requesting to borrow from friends;
- often in their overdraft;
- have little to nothing to show for all their spending;
- have no understanding of why they have no money; and
- show extreme apathy and/or disinterest in their personal finances.

I think my mum best summed up this financial archetype when she once said of my father, in that affectionate way of hers, 'He'll never have two pennies to rub together while he's got a hole in his arse.'

The Consumer Carousel

You don't have to travel far to find the person who enjoys riding the consumer carousel. If you live somewhere within the Western hemisphere, you probably have to look no further than a mirror. The vast majority of us have a strong, almost obsessive predilection toward this form of financial idiocy. It seems as though the only way we can pass the time, smother the boredom of life, self-actualise, is by buying stuff. Fromm, the great twentieth-century philosopher and psychologist, warned us of the dangers of finding fulfilment through material acquisitions. He made it explicitly clear that if we attempted to anchor our self-worth to material possessions we would eventually become passive, unproductive, mindless consumers.

> With an increase in civilization, functional property in things increases. The individual may have several suits or dresses, a house, labor-saving devices, radio and television machines, record players and recordings, books, tennis rackets, a pair of skis … When having has primarily the function of satisfying the need for ever-increasing consumption, it ceases to be a

condition for more being but basically no different from 'keeping-possessions'.

Erich Fromm
The Art of Being

Thus we become hollow acquirers and keepers of possessions. Of course, his words of wisdom have largely gone unnoticed. Shame that.

So what does it look like to ride the consumer carousel? This is the person who lives from one material acquisition to the next. Unlike the person who has to have the next best thing, they acquire without rhyme or reason and their spending habits are as unpredictable as the roll of a die. You've probably heard that old saying about working to live, not living to work. Well, the archetype of this form of financial idiocy lives to consume. Their time is spent on a narrow range of activities which include: (1) working; (2) deciding what to buy next with the money they've just earned; (3) buying the thing; and, going back to (1) again.

Having spent a number of years on the frontline in the war on education I have watched many young people waste their time and money riding the consumer carousel. And I've marvelled at their fickle susceptibility to the changing winds of fashion. It's as Jack Cade said of the vacillating allegiances of the mob, 'Was ever feather so lightly blown to and fro as this multitude?'[8] One minute they want this, the next minute that, ten minutes later something else. I've seen students chop and change trainers with frightening frequency; and these trainers aren't cheap pairs of

---

[8] Shakespeare, *Henry VI*, Part 2.

pumps off the market – we're talking £100+ per pair. I can recall a student walking into the classroom to much social fanfare. When I asked what was going on, one of his peers whispered, 'He's got the latest Balenciagas'. What the hell's that? I thought. A viral infection? Apparently Balenciaga is a super-exclusive trainer brand that retail for – are you sitting down? – £500 a pair! (I bet they're still made in a sweatshop.)

Many a time I've repeatedly had to remind (and on some occasions reprimand) my students that classroom time is not supposed to be spent searching the internet for the latest sneakers, or mobile phone, or whatever other consumer item is currently in vogue.

Though it is true that the consumer carousel caters to all ages, I've noticed that the passengers usually get hooked early. Maybe a parent, peer or capitalist lures them onto the back of one of those psychotic-looking plastic horses for a ride. Once they've straddled a giddy-up and the ride starts, they quickly become intoxicated by the endless thrill of the up and down and the round and round. Never do they question the purpose of the ride because their thoughts are rendered inaudible by the laughs and jeers of other riders. This accounts for why so few people ever get off the consumer carousel.

The Money Go-round

The person bobbing up and down and whizzing round and round on the consumer carousel can, at a distance, present a happy demeanour. Sad, deluded hedonists though they indubitably are, once they've bought that thing they so desired they can ride a dopamine high for weeks at a time. And because they're always buying, they're nearly always high – the inveterate dope addicts. By contrast the person on the money go-round more often than not strikes a forlorn and melancholy figure, for this form of financial idiocy is a singularly monotonous one, requiring the participant to pass up opportunities to enjoy life so they can endlessly chase after money.

I've known many people on the money go-round; I nearly had a go myself once. What I noticed, with my amateur anthropological eye, was that they all shared a single defining characteristic: they were never satisfied. No matter how much they earned, how big their pay packets, they always wanted more; they could never get enough, never ease the itch of wanting more. And mostly they weren't wealthy, though this does seem somewhat paradoxical considering the nature of their endeavour – viz. to grab as much cash and make as big a stash as they could. Clearly they weren't familiar with that age-old axiom: the more you earn, the more you spend.

I've often wondered what psychological malfunction could be driving people on the money go-round other than never being satisfied. While filching some credible words to support my contentions, I serendipitously stumbled on a passage written by the greatest sociologist known to mankind. This is what Karl Marx had to say on the matter of money:

> That which exists for me through the medium of *money*, that which I can pay for (i.e., which money can buy), that *am I*, the possessor of money. My own power is as great as the power of money. The properties of money are my own (the possessor's) properties and faculties. What I *am* and *can do* is, therefore, not at all determined by my individuality. I *am* ugly, but I can buy the

most beautiful woman for myself. Consequently, I am not *ugly*, for the effect of *ugliness*, its power to repel, is annulled by money. As an individual I am *lame*, but money provides me with twenty-four legs. Therefore, I am not lame. I am a detestable, dishonourable, unscrupulous and stupid man, but money is honoured and so also is its possessor. Money is the highest good, and so its possessor is good. Besides, money saves me the trouble of being dishonest; therefore, I am presumed honest. I am *stupid*, but since money is the *real mind* of all things, how should its possessor be stupid? Moreover, he can buy talented people for himself, and is not he who has power over the talented more talented than they? I who can have, through the power of money, *everything* for which the human heart longs, do I not possess all human abilities? Does not my money, therefore, transform all my incapacities into their opposites?

Karl Marx
'Money' in *Economic and Philosophical Manuscripts*

Tips, Tricks and Tools

In this section I have compiled a comprehensive list of practical tips, tricks and tools for your consideration. If applied, they can help you to:

1. save money on life's necessities;
2. become aware of unhealthy spending habits;
3. cut back on superfluous spending;
4. develop a saver's mindset;
5. build a financial safety net;
6. cure the disease of debt;
7. understand the different mortgage products so that you can select the one most appropriate for your needs; and
8. exploit untapped opportunities to develop a secondary income.

At a glance you will notice that the tips, trick and tools are relatively simple in nature and unencumbered of technical jargon. I have in no way tried to reinvent the money management wheel. I can posit a perfectly sound reason for this. That reason: it is the simple methods such as the ones featured below that really do work and achieve the desired results. If I were to smear my discussion in an obfuscating sludge of technical terminologies and gab on about complex capital investment tactics, tax-exempt offshore saving options or algorithmically traded mutual funds, most people would not feel competent or comfortable getting involved in these kinds of complicated, and often risky, fiscal affairs; and rightly so. This would then completely defeat the object of this entire enterprise: to help ordinary people improve their financial situation.

It is my firm belief that the majority of people aren't really all that interested in becoming the next king or queen of capitalism and that, in fact, they just want to be able to manage their money better, keep out of debt and find ways of saving on the things they don't want to buy, but must out of necessity, so that they have more to spend on the things they do want to buy. After all, would it not be better if you could save forty quid a month on, say, a utility bill, and instead have a bit extra to take your loved one(s) out to the movies, or a meal at a restaurant? Or, as I did, reduce your mortgage by enough so that, if you so chose, you could drop down a day at work?

Another reason why I have endeavoured to keep the tips, tricks and tools nice and simple is so that you, penny-pinching protégé, are able to implement them immediately. This is the leading quality of this entire enterprise. For example, you could, within seconds of making acquaintance with, say, the concept of runaway spending (see **Tip 3**), identify this pernicious practice and take active steps to stamp it out thus saving yourself hundreds, possibly even thousands, of pounds a year.

So together let's take a look at what's on offer. Hand in hand it'll be my pleasure and honour to walk you through each tip, trick and tool. As we meander at a pleasant pace along this path to financial enlightenment, I'll provide you with a brief explanation of how they might be implemented and how they can be best applied to maximise their effectiveness. Remember, only use what you feel will work for you. This is not a one-size-fits-all gig. Also, I would encourage you to keep your enthusiasm on a tight leash. By that I mean, don't try to implement every single piece of advice at once. This is almost destined to result in failure. I would suggest instead slowly integrating those tips, tricks and tools that are applicable to your current financial situation.

Oh, I nearly forgot, before we set off professional protocol necessitates that I conclude with a peppy motivational pick-me-up. Here goes.

If it's at all possible, do try to have a bit of fun with this. After all, soon worms will be converting you into compost and nothing much will matter then.

Tip 1: Monitoring Expenditure

What gets measured gets managed.

Peter Drucker

Have you ever had the experience of checking your account only to find in it significantly less than anticipated? 'But I'm sure I had two hundred quid left!' you say to the dispassionate cash machine, while scratching your head bald. And what comes next? That sinking-heart feeling: 'Now I won't be able to treat the kids to that trip to the zoo I promised them.' This is soon accompanied by confusion: 'Where's my money? But I could've sworn I had two hundred!' The moment the sour truth sinks in, blind rage takes hold and you fire off a volley of wild-ass allegations: 'Someone's taken money out of my account!' ... 'The bank must've buggered up!' ... 'The wife's done a supermarket sweep through Primark again!'

But as you'll soon come to realise – again! – the mystery fraudster, the bank and your wife are all innocent. You're the guilty one because you overspent.

Why does this happen? Because we humans are wonderful at forgetting, that's why. We shouldn't be too hard on ourselves, though, as this is a natural predisposition of our species, and for some things it's pretty damn useful. For example, forgetting the traumatic ordeal of childbirth is probably a good thing. If mothers could recall with perfect clarity the agony of the first experience, it's doubtful they'd consciously do it again. Thus many of us owe our existence to forgetfulness (that and alcohol, of course). A lapse in memory can also explain why, after completing a marathon, with sore feet, chronic fatigue and the resolve never to do it again, that very same person will be back in training a year later for their *next* marathon.

Forgetfulness in many other domains of life, however, is most emphatically a bad thing and it can lead to unhealthy behaviour and, ultimately, personal ruin. Next time you cross paths with a fat person ask them when they last ate. Bet they either say: 'Can't remember', or, 'Oh' (wiping the chocolate stains from their lips) 'ages ago.' Or the next time you see one of those sorry specimens stumble out of the betting shop try enquiring how long it's been since they last lost a bet. 'Lost!' they'll fire back indignantly, 'I almost very nearly never lose.'

These are, I concede, extreme examples of the human tendency to forget. However, people in their overdraft, who routinely overspend, or those who have less in their account than they remembered, usually exhibit similar sieve-like memories. If allowed to persist this seemingly innocuous oversight could result in accounting calamity. An excellent, almost foolproof method of safeguarding against financial forgetfulness is to chronicle and track expenditure.

Tracking is an immensely powerful tool, and it's easy and cheap to do. Here's some advice on a selection of the simplest forms of tracking available. I'll begin with an anecdote.

When I went through a spate of checking my account to find considerably less than anticipated, I decided – taking the most primitive option – to invest in a little notebook. I popped into a stationery shop and sourced a notebook that was as wide as a debit card but twice as deep. Why so specific with the measurements you ask? Firstly, when I cut it in half I was effectively getting two notebooks for the price of one (a penny-pincher can never turn down the chance to make a saving). Secondly, once halved, it fitted nicely in my wallet and I could take it everywhere I went – but more importantly it went everywhere my debit card went.

Of course, attempting to keep a mental record of the many transactions made throughout the day is subject to corruption and distortion. The brain's short-term memory can only hold about seven 'pieces' of information, so your chances of remembering everything you purchased while out shopping, including the exact prices of the things bought, is slim. By the time it comes to writing them all down when we get home or before tucking up for the night, we will probably have forgotten fifty per cent of everything we purchased, and the prices of those things we *do* remember will have become blurred.

Having a cash book handy whenever you go shopping makes it easy to quickly note your expenditures. Calculating costs and deductions moments after they've taken place makes it nigh on impossible to lose track of your account balance. Below is an example of how I used to document transactions and outgoings:

Date of purchase	Purchase made	Subtract from total
26-01-16	Coffee and cake: £5.00	~~£250 - £5 = £245~~ remaining
28-01-16	Book from Waterstones: £15.00	~~£245 - £15 = £230~~ remaining
03-02-16	Lunch: £30	~~£230 - £30 = £200~~ remaining
08-02-16	Petrol: £25	£200 - £25 = £175

I think you get the picture.

As you can see from this example, for a couple of quid (the cost of the notebook), we can competently and accurately track expenditure and receive immediate feedback in the process. Using this simple tool enables you to know the date you made a purchase, what that purchase was, how much the purchase cost and, most importantly, the remaining balance in your account. By making use of this simple method of financial tracking we will never again suffer the frustration of having to argue with a cash machine over the credibility of its powers of accounting – unless, of course, the fraudster, bank or wife really has been fiddling you.

Tracking as a means of detecting fraud

This monitoring system also serves as an early detection device against acts of fraud. It is not uncommon nowadays for credit cards to be cloned and funds drawn from them without the account holder's knowledge. The crooks who engage in these clandestine acts of criminality are frighteningly crafty: instead of making large purchases, which would attract unwanted attention, they often initially make only minor purchases on the stolen card and, if the card is not cancelled, continue to spend. I read a case about a man who, when it came to light that his card had been cloned, had been fleeced of over ten thousand pounds in almost ten years. This is far less likely to happen to you if you track and monitor your expenditure.

eTracking

If pen and paper is a touch too Neolithic for you, you might prefer a technological method of tracking your expenditure. My better half (who isn't the technophobe that I am) set up an online bank account for me. At first I was sceptical, and wary of viruses and hackers infiltrating my account. Initially, in my anachronistic mind, I was convinced that everyone with access to the internet would also have access to my account (and I've seen a couple of documentaries showing laptop whizzes, while sipping flat whites in a café, casually hijacking the laptops of other customers – scary stuff!). But after getting used to it, and researching the stringent safety protocols banks follow, I have now come to the conclusion that it is not only a safe, time-efficient tool but it also enables you to monitor your finances anywhere at any time.

Once you have taken the trouble to switch to online banking, and it really isn't much trouble at all (easy for me to say), accessing your account takes seconds. Before being forced to make the transition, whenever I needed to transfer funds or check my balance I had to make a trip to the bank, which I could only ever do at the weekend. Now all I have to do is flip open my laptop, input a few passwords, and in the time it takes to prepare a cup of coffee I can access all my accounts, make transactions, transfer funds and alter direct debits, all with a few swipes of the keyboard. The wonders of modern technology never cease to amaze.

Tip 2: Have a Secret Stash

The secret stash is that small fund on the side that you plan to blow in one big consumer orgasm. It's a pot of pennies that you can spend without suffering buyer's remorse. Let's be honest, saving all the time and paying bills is not much fun. In fact in can be downright depressing and demoralising. 'What's in this for me?' you begin to ask yourself as you see your hard-earned cash find its way into someone else's pockets. And there's nothing wrong with feeling this way. It's only right that you should get to enjoy the fruits of your labours, though to do so can be difficult when you have so many other financial commitments.

For some – those of a pathological persuasion – saving can grow into an addiction. You become so committed to fattening your savings account you deprive yourself of even a morsel. Because of my all-or-nothing attitude (which today goes by other names: extremism, fanaticism and/or obsessive -compulsive disorder) I started to save excessively. While amassing shedloads of cash I'd live like a vagrant, although thankfully my obsessive-compulsive disorder never drove me to hang used tea bags from a makeshift washing line or sneak into the local swimming baths for a weekly wash. Eventually I realised that my behaviour was unhealthy. Yes, it's a good thing to pay your bills. Yes, it's a good thing to live simply. And, yes, it's a good thing to save your money. However, you ought also on occasion to treat yourself. That was when the idea of having a secret stash popped into my head.

But the problem was how to siphon off small sums before they entered the vault of my savings account, because once in there, the money was locked up as safe and secure as gold at Fort Knox.

By pure chance, while rifling through the clearance items in my local Poundstretcher (my one weekly outing), I happened upon a savings tin which perfectly suited my psychological bent: the tin was completely sealed; the only way of opening it was to use a tin opener. This inability to pop the lid and pinch a pound or two acts as an additional deterrent when discipline deserts us. But just to be on the safe side, the first thing I did when I got home was to bin the tin opener.

So how did I use this savings tin? Well, at first I didn't put much thought into it. Every time I had a leftover note – regardless of the denomination – I folded it up and popped it into the tin and promptly forgot about it. After a while I hit on an idea: whenever I visited a cash machine I would withdraw an extra ten pound note specifically for the purpose of depositing it into my secret-stash tin. Initially, it didn't occur to me to do this for a specific time frame – I simply stuffed the tin until it was full. When I couldn't cram in another note I decided to crack it open. To my shock (and my other half's – she stood as witness for the grand unveiling of my first ever secret-stash tin) I had amassed just over £1,200!

Now just to clarify something. I use a secret-stash tin alongside my main savings – it in no way impacts on my cherished three-tier system (this must always take precedence; see **Rule 2: Structure Your Accounts**). One rule I have with the secret-stash tin is a simple one: all the money within it must – *must* – be spent on a non-essential material want. How good does it feel to have one thousand two hundred superfluous pounds to splurge? *Very good, that's how.* When walking through town with that hefty wedge in your back pocket it's hard not to develop the complex of a mob boss or Wall Street banker.

The secret-stash tin can be used in many other ways. If, for example, you wanted to save up for a holiday, a birthday or Christmas, then this is a great way to ensure that you have the money when that special day comes around. I suggest you start saving about ten months out from whatever it is that you are saving for and start stashing that cash as frequently as your finances will permit. In the past I used to have a tally chart taped to the front of the tin so that I could monitor the net total. However, I put a stop to that because it deprived me of the excitement of discovering at the end how much I'd amassed (sad, I know). Now I just keep stuffing the tin until it is overflowing. If I reach this glorious moment and I don't really want anything, I buy another tin and keep going (the most I've had on the go at any one time is three).

This is but one example of how you can cultivate and grow a secret stash. Having tried numerous other methods over the years the unopenable tin is the one that works best for me. That might not be the case for you, we're all mixed bags. If, instead of stuffing crumpled denominations into a tacky tin from a bargain basement store, you would prefer a more refined approach, you can open a separate savers account to which you assign a small direct debit, otherwise known as a slush fund. Whatever method you choose, the important thing is to ensure that you maintain consistent deposits over a long period of time. And remember, if at any point liquidity dries up, as it's apt to on occasions, and things become a bit tight, don't use this as an excuse to stop saving. Simply cease depositing paper money for a while and switch to stashing pound coins instead. They still add up. I know someone who saved £3,000 in two-pound coins.

Tip 3: Curb Runaway Spending

A man is rich in proportion to the number of things he can afford to let alone.

Henry David Thoreau

Runaway spending? This is where we develop a taste for something that doesn't cost much – a packet of this, a cup of that – and what starts out as an inexpensive treat turns into a costly and hard-to-cure habit (or addiction). So as to better illustrate my point, here's an anecdotal example of runaway spending in action.

Some time back I developed a predilection for Costa coffee. Don't ask me why. The coffee's nasty and the houses out of which it is served are filthy holes populated by all manner of undesirable riff-raff. At first I purchased only one cup a week on the way to work. I considered it a well-deserved end-of-the-week Friday treat – well, that's how I justified it. This one cup of coffee cost me a mere £2.20. You'll agree that this expenditure is by no means bank-busting, not for a cashed-up Westerner. But it wasn't long before one cup became two cups, then three … then one every day and, on stressful days, two per day. (I'm reminded of the Guns N' Roses song 'Mr. Brownstone'.)

A little bit here, a little bit there can quite easily go unnoticed, just like a couple of harmless snowflakes can tumble down the side of a snow-capped mountain. One minute you're enjoying a coffee and the next you find yourself crushed under an avalanche of financial foolery! It must have been a slow afternoon at work but for some reason I decided to take a step back and scrutinise the cost of my coffee addiction. I think perhaps what inspired this action was the bin beside my desk, which was overflowing with cardboard and plastic.

Runaway spending – do the math if you dare!

Daily spending: Two coffees at £2.20 each amounts to a daily expense of £4.40 – equal to about 10 minutes of paid employment. That doesn't sound so bad. Keep reading, it will.

Weekly Spending: Over a five-day working week that £4.40 has snowballed into £22, now a single hour's earnings.

Monthly Spending: Multiplying £22 by four weeks sees us arrive at a heart palpitating sum of £88. Half a day at work each month is spent earning money for coffee! What a prat! But it gets worse.

Yearly Spending: (Warning! Whenever calculating runaway spending make sure you are seated and that there are no sharp objects to hand.) Multiplying £88 by twelve months gives us a nausea-inducing yearly spend of £1,056! The equivalent of 2.5 weeks, or 100 hours, shackled to a desk!

The fact cannot be ignored: spending £1,056 a year on coffee is outrageous. To think that a little over two working weeks' wages out of every year are wasted on coffee. Given the option what would you prefer: a daily coffee or an extra two weeks off on holiday? This prat chose the former. And what makes it worse is that the coffee isn't even that good, and it's from a large chain that is notorious for massive mark-ups, avoiding contributing to the social pot and exploiting minimum-wage workers.

The problem is, and this is why it's so easy to fall into the runaway spending trap, a couple of quid a day is barely noticeable and it doesn't tend to show up anywhere. Loose change and small denominations are buggers for slipping through the financial net. Remember Drucker's sagacious maxim: *What gets measured gets managed.* Make those simple words your mantra and never again will you be in the dark regarding your personal finances.

It is because of the seeming insignificance of the sums that runaway spending escapes radar detection and why we must develop other methods of identifying it. If you've got into the unhealthy habit of buying pointless plastic products off Amazon or buying other people's junk off eBay, because these payments go through a bank (or equivalent), these unhealthy expenditures will eventually rear their ugly heads on your bank statement. A few quid on a coffee is not so obvious.

Anyway, here's what I decided to do to try and shock myself out of this pernicious habit.

Firstly, I implemented a rule, which was: for every coffee I purchased I had to deposit an equal sum into a money tin that I kept locked in a cupboard by my desk. This is an excellent tactic because it instantly transforms the trifling sum of £4.40 into £8.80 which, from a psychological perspective, is more noticeable. Also, unlike loose change, few of us rarely have a spare ten pounds lying around each day that we can use to buy a couple of coffees with. What does this mean? We physically have to go to the cash machine and withdraw it – or pay on our card, which amounts to pretty much the same thing. Now the spending has become both *VISIBLE!* and a logistical embuggerance.

Secondly, I saved every single Costa cup that I bought. By my desk, over a couple of weeks of coffee consumption, I built a towering stack of cups that very quickly climbed to the ceiling. Yes, this got me a lot of odd looks from my colleagues, and I probably answered the question 'Why have you got a stack of Costa cups by your desk?' a hundred times, but it worked a treat! Seeing that gigantic and ever-growing stack woke me up not only to the obscene sum of money I had been wasting, but also (and more importantly) to the singularly disgusting amount of waste I had been ignorantly producing.

After two weeks, when I could no longer afford the additional payments to my desk-drawer savers tin and the tower of cups threatened collapse, I stopped drinking Costa coffee – forever! But I continued to save the £4.40, which I plan to use to subsidise my measly government pension when I eventually retire (if the government has anything to do with it, however, doubtful will the day ever come).

Tip 4: The Law of Incremental Accumulation (LIA)

The LIA is, in some ways, like gravitational attraction: it holds many of the *Penny-Pinchers'* methods together. It transcends boundaries and permeates the principles of money management. I aim to explain and showcase its potential power and – more importantly – how it can be effectively applied. To give one simple example, LIA can clearly be seen in action with the secret-stash tin (see above): popping away the occasional £10 or £20 note, trifling denominations in themselves, can, over time, accumulate into rather sizeable sums. LIA is also at work in the example I gave of runaway spending – little bits here and there lead to a lot over time – albeit negatively.

The one downside with LIA is that it can be slow to deliver tangible results. Let me give you an example. I decided one day that I no longer wanted to give as much money as I was to my electricity supplier – my money is, after all, better off in my pocket than it is in theirs. So I looked at how much I was presently spending on electricity. The monthly average and yearly overall totals were compiled, written down and placed somewhere prominent such as the kitchen noticeboard (see **Tip 7: Make it *VISIBLE!***). I then analysed where I might be using more electricity than I needed to. Once I'd identified where I could reduce electricity consumption, I implemented my action plan:

- Turn off all appliances at the wall when they are not in use.
- Only switch lights on in rooms that are occupied.
- Change all light bulbs to energy-efficient bulbs (however much it costs to replace the bulbs must be deducted from the overall net saving).
- Use electric guitar amplifier for one practice session as opposed to two (each practice session lasts for approximately 1 hour).
- Turn the electric hobs down when cooking. (My other half is a nightmare for this; when the pasta is boiling away she insists on keeping the heat cranked up full whack even though the water will comfortably continue to simmer at less than half the heat. Water, I keep telling her, cannot exceed 100°C!)
- Reduce time in the shower to two minutes as opposed to four (and sometimes much more).
- Charge mobile phone and any other electronic device at work.

I strictly maintained these energy conservation habits for a month so as to get an accurate picture of the monthly bill. After comparing past bills to the new one I was pleased to see that I'd made a saving of £7.20. Arguably a pittance by today's standards, but it's worth remembering that by implementing the above action plan I was able to reduce my electricity bill by over 22%. Imagine if you could reduce every bill by as much? Now we're talking big savings. All those incremental adjustments to my electricity usage, and being reminded of it daily by the figures on the noticeboard, literally paid off. In itself, £7.20 isn't enough to secure a pad on Lake Garda, I know. However, it is, undeniably, £7.20 extra in my pocket every month to spend on what I want. And if you were to scrutinise this seemingly nominal sum through the rose-tinted lenses of LIA, you will see a yearly saving of around £86.

Now, what I tend to do in situations such as this is, instead of allowing this small saving to be engulfed by the monthly bills where little to no benefit will be noticed, I withdraw the sum and stash it in a secret-stash tin. As it was previously budgeted for anyway within my necessary outgoings it will not be missed. However, at the end of the year when I crack open my secret-stash tin it will then be noticed and much appreciated. To think, if £7.20 were saved on each of the utilities – water, gas, electricity – that would equate to around £22 per month or £260 over the year.

Here are some other ways I use LIA to save money on things I don't want to pay for so that I have more to spend on things I do. Warning! Some of these suggestions may appear a little *eccentric*.

(a) water down household cleaning/cosmetic products – washing-up liquid, antibacterial cleaners, body wash (etc.) – to make them go further.
    This is nothing new, I know. Take washing-up liquid. It's so potent that pouring about a tenth of it into a bottle of similar volume and then diluting the remaining ninth with water does not diminish its ability to make those glasses glisten. By doing

this I can make one bottle last for more than five. Again, the saving on this one item is insubstantial, but doing it consistently could reduce your monthly shopping bill by £20 or more.

(b) Car-sharing (if possible).
My partner and I both car share – primarily for environmental reasons – and together we save £60 a month. An added bonus to car-sharing is that you also save on general automotive wear and tear. Fewer miles translates to fewer tyres, fewer filters and fewer head gaskets.

(c) Get your bank to round up your balance and put the difference in a savings account.
My bank has this nifty initiative called 'save the pennies' – which is quite appropriate and in keeping with the *Penny-Pinchers*' ethos. It works like this. Every time you make a transaction on your card the sum total of the spend is rounded up to the nearest pound and that excess, which will never exceed £0.99, is automatically deposited into a savers account. Simple though this intervention is it's a clever little way to siphon off some superfluous pennies. See example below:

Spent on debit card	Rounded up to nearest £ and transferred to savings	Total deduction shown on statement
Lunch £4.49	£0.51	£5.00
Coffee £2.10	£0.90	£3.00
	£1.41 saved	

(d) Buy in bulk!

I stumbled on the superior savings that can be made when buying in bulk by accident. While purchasing my preferred body wash offline – one of those expensive eco-friendly, no harmful chemicals, no animal testing brands (things that, for some strange reason, you've got to pay a premium for), I noticed the same product in 5-litre tubs. The price of £30 seemed a little steep for a single purchase of body wash, I must admit. But when I crunched the numbers it transpired that I'd make an obscene saving by buying 5 litres as opposed to the usual 250ml. Incredulous? See for yourself:

- 5-litre tub retails at £30.
- 250ml bottle retails at £5.50.
- Math question for you: how many 250ml bottles of body wash could you squeeze into a 5-litre tub?
- 20 bottles – well done!
- Another math question for you: complete the following sum: 20 X £5.50.
- £110! You're getting good at this. Eat your heart out, Gödel.
- Final math question: If Sanjib goes to the shop with £110 to buy 20 bottles of body wash, each costing £5.50, but notices that there's a 5-litre tub of the same stuff for £30, how much money will he save by buying 5 litres?
- Correct! £80!
- Congratulations, you're a competent number cruncher.

And that, I think you'll agree, is a hefty saving and one not to be snubbed.

But wait, there's more benefits to buying in bulk. In the example given above, one 5-litre tub, even though it contains equal volume of body wash, requires ten times less plastic than twenty 250ml bottles. And at a time when there is apparently over a trillion individual pieces of plastic polluting the sea, every reduction in waste is welcome. In addition, far fewer deliveries are required because a 5-litre tub literally lasts for months; longer still if you water it down. Fewer deliveries translates to a reduction in the size of your carbon footprint. The boons of buying in bulk abound![1]

Now it's over to you to get creative and find innovative ways of exploiting the LIA. When you do, or if you've developed some of your own methods already, I'd love to hear about them. Visit www.penny-pinchers.co.uk, share your ideas and help others on their penny-pinching journey.

Tip 5: Sign Over Power of Attorney

The first principal is that you must not fool yourself, and you are the easiest person to fool.

Richard P. Feynman

If your self-discipline is as robust as a well-dunked digestive biscuit, then this might just be the trick you've been looking for.

---

[1] Shortly after penning this paragraph I sold the second car and bought a bike – probably the best decision I've made in years. I now not only save loads of money (the price of maintaining a pushbike is an order of magnitude less than that of a car), and no longer have to suffer seeing my sweet time trickle away in commuter traffic, but I enjoy the almost unlimited freedom that comes with a bike and the additional exercise: cycling is good both for your health and the environment.

Scenario: you're in a spot of financial trouble. Your outgoings exceed your incomings, you're slowly running up more and more debt and you're always in your overdraft. So what should you do about it? As I see it, there are only two options available and only one of them is worth taking:

(1) Do as the ostrich purportedly does.

(2) Take action: formulate a sound strategy around a clearly defined kernel and with diligence and sustained determination proceed by degrees to extricate yourself from your financial funk.

So I'm guessing that I'm addressing those readers who selected option (2). Now, you probably want to know how best to take action so that you can overcome your financial predicament. Here is a method which may help.

Open a joint bank account with a responsible family member where they – not you – have controlling power over your expenditure.

I acknowledge that this might not seem like the solution for a mature adult, but if you are a mature adult who spends like an irresponsible teenager, then an extreme measure is certainly required – and if you've exhausted all other solutions, then why not give this one a shot? What've you got to lose?

When I first opened a savings account it had to be a joint account with my dear ma because I was only twelve. I could deposit money into the account, watch it grow and dream of one day going into business with Warren Buffett, but only Mother could make withdrawals. I still used that account in my twenties! That wasn't because I had the spending discipline of an inveterate crack addict; I simply could never be bothered to change it. When I got a full-time job I set up a direct debit to deposit a substantial portion of each month's wage into that joint account. If ever I overspent from my current account (which at the time had no overdraft) I had to ring up Mum and ask her to release some savings. An embarrassing position to be in when you're supposed to be both a mature adult and member of an elite military organisation – at the time I was serving in the Royal Marines. Also, to fix my financial folly Mum would have to make a trip into town to transfer the funds – thus compounding the inconvenience.

I am sure you can easily see how this acts as a preventative measure – as a *safeguard* – to runaway spending habits. If my overspending became habitual, Mum would question this unhealthy behaviour and, deeming it a problem, refuse to relinquish any cash. 'You'll just have to go without this week, son,' she'd say, struggling to disguise the undertones of disappointment in her voice. Damn, that would cut me to the quick. But sometimes you have to be cruel to be kind, right? It shouldn't come as a surprise to learn that I rarely rang home to request a bailout.

A real delinquent, of course, could quite easily circumvent their attorney by borrowing from external sources such a shady friend, their bank, or by turning to a payday loan company – or crime. But for people who fall into this category, nothing short of debtor's prison will prevent them from frittering away their money.

Tip 6: 30-Day Spending Fast

Food fasts are good for you – very good actually. Alcohol fasts (more accurately, abstentions) are good for you too. In fact, pretty much all fasts are good for you. And it is exactly true of spending fasts. So what is a spending fast? This is where for a set period of time – say, one month of the year – you do not spend a single superfluous penny. Pay the bills. Yes. Get the shopping (in accordance to your strict budget and pre-planned list). Yes. Put petrol in the car. Yes. But the fancy stuff, the fineries? NO! For one month you live like a Buddhist monk in a monastery, like a sheep herder in Afghanistan, like people used to live years ago when there wasn't myriad pointless stuff to waste money on.

You might wonder why. Why consciously impose this harsh ascetic intervention? What possible good could come from it?

Well, for those among the readership who are currently suffering financial difficulties, a spending fast will enable you to direct more money into your deficit, thus helping you to pay off those credit/store cards and/or overdraft more quickly. A spending fast also helps you to cultivate and develop monetary management discipline, endowing you with the ability to check that impulse that leads to unnecessary consumerism. In addition, a spending fast could awaken you to the materialistic trap that so many in the Western world are stuck in and blinded by. Lots of people have little to no idea how to spend their time so, to fill the gaping void that exists within them, they spend their money. The void can never be filled – not with all the gadgets, clothes, cars or jewellery in the world. We all intrinsically know that the pleasure we receive from buying is a brief, short-lived experience (the buyer's high), which leads only to one thing – buying more, and more, and more ad infinitum.

I see this self-perpetuating cycle time and again. From the outside you can clearly see how dangerous this behaviour is and also how the psychological instability that is its root cause leads to the proliferation and exacerbation of spending for spending's sake. An acquaintance of mine developed a taste – I should say more accurately, an *addiction* – for exclusive wristwatches. 'Exclusive' is another word for 'expensive', by the way. My question was always how many watches does one man need? I thought it was one but apparently there is no established number. This acquaintance of mine acquired a collection of over twenty watches – the average price of each one: £2,000. Do the maths! I know, crazy, isn't it? He'd waxed forty grand on what effectively were objects to bolster social prestige and which would spend the majority of their time locked away in a safe slowly depreciating in value.

Now, it's not for me to say what people should or shouldn't spend their money on. But what piqued my curiosity was the underlying addiction behind these pointless acquisitions, and from where exactly it manifested. What drove this obsessive and wholly unnecessary compulsion? This is how the process would perpetuate itself: before making a substantial purchase – which always involved a lot of umming and ahhing, discussion and indecision about exactly what brand of watch was best to buy – this individual would say, after having finally made a decision, 'This is the best watch in the world. No other watch compares. I'll never need another. This is the last one' … and so on. But after a few months, the shine of this new indulgence would have dulled considerably and there'd be whisperings of trading it in (at a serious financial loss) for a different timepiece – presumably the best *best* watch in the world.

Granted, for most people their materialistic vice is not a watch fettered to a four-figure price tag. However, the desire to keep up with the latest fashion, the Joneses, or the next new technological innovation, probably amounts to the same expenditure as an exclusive timepiece over the course of a year. A spending fast can help combat (or at the very least arrest) this behaviour – and if you exercise the requisite discipline to see it through for the full thirty days, maybe bring home the realisation that happiness does not exist in materialistic acquisitions. Ultimately this will be a good thing as your life will be enlightened by the age-old axiom: the best things in life are free.

Spending-fast durations

The length of a spending fast could range from a full year to as little as a single weekend. The fasting length selected depends on a person's fiscal habits. For example, for a person who is addicted to consumerism, lasting an entire weekend without spending a penny would be a praiseworthy achievement. A short weekend spending fast to the extreme consumer can act like that much-needed slap to the face, waking them to their life of wanton excess. Once they realise that life is actually more pleasant when they're not wasting it buying pointless overpriced stuff, they may consider increasing the fasting period or decide to tighten the leash and rein in their rabid spending practices.

I must confess, I used to be an extreme consumer, incapable of remaining cooped up indoors over the weekend. To avoid a psychological meltdown, I had to go out to a café or an eatery or do something that involved spending. I lived like that for years until I woke up to the waste of time and wealth. Over that period of time I must have squandered thousands on ... what? Coffee? Overpriced food? Stuff? Once I realised my mistake I began enforcing short weekend fasts, just one a month to begin with. At first I found it surprisingly challenging to last forty-eight hours without scuttling off to my local café or whiling away an afternoon in a bookshop. At the end of my first weekend fast I realised that I'd in fact formed a kind of addiction which proved to be very difficult to break. However, when it eventually dawned on me that in order to have a good time I didn't need to be out and about, spending money unnecessarily, I became aware of a number of positive outcomes during those weekends that I fasted. These outcomes included:

- A noticeable spike in levels of productivity. When you're not driving here, there and everywhere and wasting hours in cafés or restaurants you're bound to have more time to dedicate to other activities and pursuits.
- The number of debit card transactions dropped precipitously. On comparing and contrasting the number of debits made to my account over non-fasting weekends and fasting weekends I calculated a 90% decrease. Though this is an obvious outcome to be expected, it still acted as fuel to my motivational fire.
- I began engaging in other activities – such as walking, cycling, reading, playing the guitar – that were not only cost-free but were more enjoyable and physically/intellectually/musically beneficial.

- I found that I had more money at the end of each month, which was a good thing because at the time I was neck-deep in debt.

Over the years I've trained myself to be able to fast for months at a time. The longest I've gone without spending is an entire year. Yep, you read that right: 365 days and not one unnecessary promissory note exchanged. Okay, I wasn't quite as strict as I'm making out. I just wanted to impress you. For a fast of this duration instead of prohibiting any and all pecuniary pleasures – such as a coffee and croissant at my local – I enforced an embargo on all spends of a substantial size. For example, I said to myself: over the next twelve months I am strictly forbidden from spending, on any single item, more than £25 and I am only allowed to spend that at the end of each month. The rules applied to substantial fasts – six or more months – are not as constricting as they would be for shorter ones.

Now I know that to the ears of some readers this will smack somewhat of sadomasochism – tyrannical and oppressive even. Withdrawing completely from all economic activity can seem like being deposited in the Stone Age with our ape-like ancestors. There might well be some truth in this assessment, but that doesn't mean it's a bad thing. In fact, I can assure you that abstaining from consumerism, which is quite possibly the single most primitive way to spend one's time, is the antithesis of bad. From my experience of fasting for a full year I can attest to the economic emancipating effects conferred. Truly, it is liberating not to be harassed by the urges that compel the consumer to spend and buy. Furthermore, fasting provides you with a new

153

perspective – you get to see the base consumer for the pig-ignorant, hedonistic, self-indulgent beast that they are.

All I ask is, before you turn your nose up and dismiss spending fasts out of hand, give it a go. You have nothing to lose but your chains. You have a world to win.

In the table below I have produced a range of spending-fast suggestions. You can modify them to suit your lifestyle. But, remember, it would be pointless if the fast was so prohibitively restrictive that you quit before you even got started, or found it so unpleasant that you resolve never to do it again. By comparison, if you repealed the rules and reduced them to insignificance, such that no difference to your spending habits was made, the fast would be rendered ineffective. The consequence? No pecuniary benefit conferred.

So, before making any modifications, assess your current spending habits and powers of personal discipline. If you're an incurable consumer coupled with the self-control of a dog on heat, consider easing the rules. However, they still need to present a challenge; no point otherwise.

Single weekend	As this is the shortest duration fast it is the strictest. For the entire weekend – say from close of play Friday to Monday morning – you should abstain from spending a single penny on anything other than essentials.
One month	Over the course of one month you are forbidden to spend any money on anything but essentials.

Six months	This is a little less severe. While you are permitted to make small purchases no greater than £25, you may do so only once a month; also, ensure to use paper as opposed to plastic as this will prevent overspending. I advise that prior to embarking on a six-month fast, you decide which week within the month you plan to treat yourself and stick rigidly to it.
One year	The rules for the year-long fast are the same as for the six-month fast.

If you plucked up the courage to try one of the above spending fasts, irrespective of whether you lasted the duration or not, congratulations! They're a lot harder than they look. I'd like to hear about your experiences – if you found the fast useful or too easy/difficult, and if it made a noticeable difference to your financial situation. Visit www.penny-pinchers.co.uk.

Tip 7: Make it *VISIBLE!*

This is a hugely important aspect of maintaining financial health. Living in a state of denial over your financial affairs or refusing to track and chart the flow of money into and out of your account will – WILL! – eventually result in catastrophe. Believe me, I'm talking from personal experience.

When I got into financial difficulty by not paying attention to runaway spending habits, I dug out all my bank statements and, armed with a pink highlighter, I put a line through every unnecessary transaction of the previous month. After ten minutes of rampant highlighting the paper was more pink than white. I was utterly staggered by the obscene level of wastage. I'd spent: £200 on books (no one can read two hundred quid's worth of books in a month, especially not me because I am a shockingly slow reader); nearly £300 in a supermarket (I was serving in the military at the time and we were provided with three free meals a day); over £150 on coffee – yes, on coffee! In a month! (Until I saw it with my own eyes I wouldn't have thought this possible either.)

I remember slumping back in my chair, bank statement in one hand, smoking highlighter in the other, asking myself what the hell I had been playing at. Every single transaction I made was unnecessary. All just grotesque wastage and excessive consumption. Granted, the capitalists loved me – I was their consumerist ideal, a mindless idiot who spent money without a second's thought – but I knew this behaviour was extremely unhealthy and I immediately moved to put a stop to it. Here's what I did.

History, if you pay attention, can teach you a number of valuable lessons. Before I took active steps to stem the flood of financial transactions that flowed thick and fast from my account I considered taking the approach of a nineteenth-century cane-brandishing headmaster. But then I remembered that the rod rarely brings about the results desired; usually it just provokes anger and resentment. When the American government tried to cure its citizens of their thirst for alcohol by enforcing strict prohibition, their ill-conceived laws only succeeded in giving rise to one of the worst spates of crime and civil disobedience in the country's history. In this enormously costly and disruptive social experiment the US government proved one thing: people don't like to be *told* what to do. I'm no different and I'm sure you're not. So I decided against enforcing draconian anti-spending restrictions on myself knowing full well they'd only piss off my rebellious side.

Thus I considered applying a bit of psychological tact. I decided to allow myself to continue spending on the proviso that I documented all transactions and made them visible. Also, I enforced budgetary restrictions and switched from using credit cards to cash.

By adopting this approach I could still enjoy the occasional coffee with a friend and buy a book (when I'd finished all those unread titles). And even though I still had to stick to some pretty strict budgetary caps, it didn't really feel that way. Examples of those caps included going for a coffee only on Fridays and Saturdays rather than every day (sometimes twice a day), or only buying a new book when – and only when – I'd finished the one I was reading.

In conjunction with these positive steps I enforced a complete ban on the purchase of food from supermarkets. In fact I went so far as to slap myself with a restraining order that prevented me from going within one hundred metres of one. I had to eat the food that was provided courtesy of the Ministry of Defence, regardless of how disgusting and nutritionally deficient it was. While forcing greasy shepherd's pie into my maw, I told myself, 'This is gonna save you three hundred quid a month!'

Little did I know at the time but by enforcing these lifestyle restrictions I'd implemented a self-discipline strengthening exercise espoused by Seneca. To prepare ourselves for hardship, should it come knocking without warning, and to bring about an appreciation of creature comforts, he advises that we

> Set aside a certain number of days, during which you shall be content with the scantiest and cheapest fare, with course and rough dress, saying to yourself the while: "Is this the condition that I feared?'

VISIBILITY! Board

My final tactic was to make every single transaction VISIBLE! This was by far one of the most potent methods of bringing about behaviour change. To make my spending visible I 'acquired' (aka misappropriated from a stationery cupboard) a two-by-two-foot piece of dry-wipe whiteboard and a black marker. At the top of what I christened the '*VISIBILITY!* Board' (ensuring to use the most garish and conspicuous colour pen possible) I wrote the date that I got paid, the amount HMG deemed I was worth (apparently merely £1,200) and, after deducting all bills and necessary outgoings, exactly how much disposable cash I had remaining for the month.

The embuggerance of bills! And the importance of accounting accuracy

Few people look forward to paying their bills. Scratch that – *no one* looks forward to paying their bills. Bills are bastards and they are a burden upon our backs which we must carry from the cradle to the grave. How depressing! But of course we can lighten the load so that they don't slow us down as much. We already discussed some methods of reducing bills in the chapter on Financial Strategy (for a refresh turn back to page 9).

What I really want to draw your awareness to here is how bills can negatively impact on accounting accuracy, and accuracy is king when it comes to the *VISIBILITY!* Board.

Some companies are very irritating – like my car insurance company, for example. For reasons that still remain a mystery they cannot transact the direct debit until halfway through the month. This is frustrating for people who are either on a tight budget or who are making use of a *VISIBILITY!* Board. For if that mid-monthly bill slips your mind, it can throw your calculations out of whack, and it usually does so when you least expect it. When I was really poor, much poorer than I am now, and lived on a shoestring budget, £30 could be the difference between getting through the month in credit – or not.

I remember once forgetting to factor my mid-monthly car insurance bill into my calculations and being inadvertently lulled into a false sense of wealth. It wasn't until after a rather decadent meal at an Italian restaurant (where I ordered double helpings of dessert – by god, those profiteroles were to die for!) that I realised I still had to pay for the privilege of protecting other motorists. I paid my penance for that blunder: two weeks in isolation on bread and water.

To prevent this unfortunate situation from happening again I made minor adjustments to the format of the *VISIBILITY!* Board. On the left-hand side of the board I made a list of every direct debit and necessary outgoing, ensuring to total them at the bottom. When I received that small sack of monkey nuts from the MOD, I immediately divvied out the nuts that belonged to Bill and his many mates while setting aside a little stash for a rainy day and a pocketful to nibble on now.

When all your outgoings, deductions and remaining cash calculations are accurately put up on the *VISIBILITY!* Board, it's ready to rock and roll. What's left to do now is to position it in a prominent place. Of course, there's no use going to all this trouble, then sticking your board up in the loft. I put mine right by my bed so that I could see it before I went to sleep (that way my dreams would be haunted by the spectre of financial mismanagement) and as soon as I woke up.

Every single time I bought something I would write it down on the board, making sure to accurately subtract from the total. By doing this I received instant and *VISIBLE!* feedback on the three most important indicators of my current financial status:

(1) how much money I have in my account right now
(2) how much I have left remaining for the month
(3) inappropriate or excessive spending trends

See below example of how I used a *VISIBILITY* Board to *expose* money management malpractice and *improve* accounting.

VISIBILITY! Board

Monthly Expenditure

Pay Total = £1,200

Total Outgoings = £675 –

Savings Account = £250 –

Spending money after deductions and savings = £275

1/7/2021 -£25 (meal out)

R £250

1/7/2021 -£50 (new pair of trainers)

R £200

2/7/2021 -£25 (meal out)

R £175

2/72021 -£10 (mum's b-day present)

R £165

3/7/2021 -£25 (meal out)

R £140

4/7/2021 -£10 (guitar strings)

R £130

5/7/2021 -£25 (meal out)

R £105

6/7/2021 -£8.50 (coffee and cake)

Monthly Outgoings

Mortgage = £500

Home insurance = £20

Utilities = £100

Car insurance = £20

Phone contract = £20

TV licence = £15

Total outgoings = £675

Savings Accounts

Account 1 = £125

Account 2 = £75

Account 3 = £50

Total savings = £250

Now if you cast your eyes to the monthly expenditure column on the *VISIBILITY!* Board, you will no doubt have noticed a reoccurring deduction which clearly indicates excessive spending. No one needs to eat out that often; it's just plain lazy and it's bad for your health. Armed with this information you can make changes to your behaviour, which will bring about a number of positives – a fatter bank balance and slimmer waist being the most obvious.

Did you know that we at *Penny-Pinchers* sell our very own *VISIBILITY!* Boards? You didn't! Where've you been? Yes, we sell them and they're brilliant. They have been designed with the penny-pincher in mind. Each board is sectioned off in a way similar to the example above – only much better, of course – so that you don't have to concern yourself with such complications. If you are interested in owning your very own *VISIBILITY!* Boards just pop on to the website www.penny-pinchers.co.uk and you'll find them in our store.

Alternatively, save your pennies and create your own *VISIBILITY!* Board for free. Two ways of doing this include:

1) appropriate a 2-foot-by-2-foot square of laminated MDF; 2) daub half a tin of black paint on a patch of unproductive wall and, after procuring a packet of chalk sticks, get accounting.

Tip 8: Treasure Trove

Think of this part as one of those kitchen drawers in which we stick our knick-knacks, odds and sods and any other unwanted crap. Under Tip 8: Treasure Trove you will discover an extensive range of money-saving ideas. Some will be of use to you, others won't. Implement what works, discard what doesn't.

Gym membership

Do you currently pay an annual gym membership? Well, if you are looking to tighten your financial belt you may be able to do so by cancelling that gym membership while also improving your fitness. 'Hold on a second, that makes no sense. You're telling me I can cancel my gym membership, save money *and* improve my fitness?' That is precisely what I'm saying. Allow me to explain.

I worked in a gym for a year before I quit because the pay was crap and the job was the personification of monotony. Apparently the gym's books boasted that it had a whopping 3,000 paying members – that's members who pay a monthly fee of £25 via direct debit. Yet in the nine months of my employment, which saw me work every conceivable antisocial shift pattern you could possibly imagine, I encountered only about 150 different people – at a push 200. Where were the other 2,750 paying members? Granted, some of those memberships were attributed to corporate partnerships, but they wouldn't have accounted for more than 500. So all said and done there were anywhere between 2,000 and 2,250 people paying for a membership that they weren't using (or using it infrequently – probably only on 1st January).

This was great for the gym because we enjoyed a substantial revenue stream (more like a river) and our equipment got very little use. However, I would often think of all those people willingly wasting their money on something they were not making use of. To me it defies comprehension. It wouldn't have surprised me if a lot of those people didn't even know they were still paying a £25 monthly direct debit. But this behaviour, I later learned, is quite common. A recent statistic published in a national newspaper highlighted that Britons waste a colossal £558 million a year on unused gym memberships.[2] In addition, the report claimed that more than one in 10 members said they do not attend the gym from one year to the next.

It is a widely held belief that if you want to improve your fitness, then you absolutely must get yourself down to the nearest gym. This is pure poppycock.

Drawing from the deep well of my many years of experience in the world of health and fitness, which saw me work in numerous gyms both as an instructor and personal trainer, I can say with unflinching confidence that 95% of all gym goers waste their time. Their health would be no worse if they stayed at home on the couch. The fact is that the vast majority of gym users fail to exert themselves sufficiently to promote physiological adaptation. Curling dumb-bells, updating social media and watching TV while peddling away aimlessly are not going to stimulate the biological responses required to improve health. But it gets worse. Gyms are a veritable hive of misinformation and deleterious advice. Thus the health of many gym users actually degrades! Just to clarify: yes, I really did imply that many people become *less* healthy and *lose* fitness as a consequence of using the gym. Why is this? The reasons are manifold and to

---

[2] 'Britons waste a colossal £558 million a year on unused gym memberships' taken from a report in the Daily Mirror: www.mirror.co.uk/news/uk-news/brits-wasting-558m-unused-gym (cited online 18/1/2021).

adequately explore them would lead us astray from the concern of this book. But, to offer a glimmer of insight, so as not to leave you guessing, gym users typically retrograde in fitness due to a subtle combination of ignorance, laziness and the covetous compulsion to pursue unnatural aesthetics over health.

Now I'm not saying that gyms can't be beneficial. They obviously can – but only in the right hands. For the vast majority of users superior fitness could be obtained by jogging/cycling 3 to 4 times a week and completing a series of callisthenics at the local park. None of which costs a single dime.

So, with that said, review your current levels of participation and approach. If they fit the bill described above, cancel your gym membership. Also, while you're at it, give your bank accounts a sweep for memberships and/or subscriptions that you are no longer using and cancel them too. Do this effective immediately!

Switching accounts
My first ever bank account was with Halifax. I took a joint account out with my mum when I was about twelve (I've told you this story already). Back then we were given little blue books, which we handed over to the cashier whenever we made a deposit or withdrawal. They fed it into the maw of a machine, which after noisily munching on the book for a bit promptly spat it back out. And that's where the magic took place. The machine would make the necessary subtractions or additions. How good it felt to watch all those deposits mount up. I turned it into a competition to see how many additions I could go without making a subtraction. It's possibly these memories and I suppose habit that for years

inhibited me from seeking a better bank, a bank that paid me for being a customer and not the other way round.

I can't quite recall the circumstances under which I made the discovery, but one day I found out that my bank had been charging me £20 a month for what they called a 'reward' account. For the life of me I could not remember switching accounts but I do remember asking 'Why the hell am I paying this bank £20 a month when there are other banks offering to pay *me* to have an account with them?' At the time I was paying £240 a year for an account with Halifax, yet TSB were willing to pay me £5 a month to open an account with them and a further £5 if I made twenty card transactions throughout the month. On juggling the numbers I realised that if I switched, I would be a full £360 a year better off!

For us humans change is hard – it actually hurts – and it inevitably requires hassle. However, I happily learned that when switching accounts the bank does almost everything for you. All I had to do was make the effort to pop into my local TSB branch, wait in a queue for five minutes and tell a 'member of the team' that I wanted to transition from my current bank to them. The only inconvenience that I incurred was when I had to attend an appointment at TSB to sign some paperwork. The time it took from start to finish meant I earned about £360 (over a year) for thirty minutes of work.

As with utility companies, home/content and car insurance, we should chop and change when a better deal becomes available. Gone are the days of customer loyalty. I had car insurance through Tesco for years until I noticed that they were charging me slightly more for each renewal. One year, when the price of my insurance increased by five pounds a month, I contacted the company and asked them why, even though I'd never made a claim and I was a loyal customer. 'This is just what we do now,' the polite woman on the other end of the line said. 'Just what we do'? What does that even mean? Well what I did was change insurance companies and found one that was over fifteen pounds a month cheaper.

The moral of this story is, when it comes to banks, insurance and utilities, you absolutely must shop around for better deals. If you don't, you could well be paying hundreds, possibly even thousands, of pounds extra every year in fees or for a more expensive service. And in today's technological age finding a cheaper service could not be easier. All it requires is that we exercise a little bit of discipline and force ourselves occasionally to compare market prices. When a contract comes up for renewal DO NOT renew it automatically. Go bargain hunting first. As for bank accounts we must maintain vigilance for new offers and better deals. Lots of banks are now starting to offer one-off rewards when you switch. Coincidently, shortly after I switched to TSB, Halifax offered new customers £150 if they switched from their pre-existing bank. Suffice to say, I made the switch, took the bait, waited out the term, then promptly switched back again.

Task

Here are the steps to take to review your accounts and regular payments:

- Make a list of all your direct debits, including how much each one costs. Example: car insurance = £20; home and contents = £16; utilities = £125; etc., etc.
- Now combine those individual costs into a grand total.
- Once you've done that try to find a provider offering a better price. Write the name of the company and their price opposite your current provider.
- After you've compiled this new list add up the totals again.
- Compare what you're currently paying to what you could be paying and ask yourself if the potential saving is enough to make you want to switch provider.

Organise your accounts like an engineer and never not have enough for a bill again!

A few years back I was attending a teacher training course. During a mind-numbingly dull two hour-long lecture a fellow student and I struck-up quiet conversation. We'd clearly arrived at the same conclusion – *ergo* if we didn't seek distraction we'd inevitably slip into insanity. After exchanging the obligatory pleasantries and breaking the ice, the subject turned to matters concerning financial planning.

Now don't ask me how our conversation led us into a topical landscape arguably more arid and desolate than that of the theoretical underpinnings of applied pedagogy. My memories are too dusty to recall every step of the journey. However, my new friend, who by profession was an engineer, divulged his secret method of mitigating financial shortfalls.

But before I embark on an exposition of his method, I've got a quick question for you. Question: Have you ever been hit with a bill, expected or not, only to find that you didn't have the liquidity to absorb the financial impact? You take the car to the garage for an MOT thinking it'll breeze through no problem. But when you collect it an hour later the grease monkey slaps you with a lengthy list of mechanical faults that he absolutely *had* to fix to make the motor 'road worthy'. (Oh, how many times I've heard that!) And what you thought was going to cost a little, costs a lot. But praise be to those considerate bankers for creating the credit system! Or then there are the annual bills that, though annual (meaning you pay them every year and have been doing so for the past ten), you always forget until a reminder is stuffed through the letterbox. And why is it that those reminders come knocking when we're foundering on the financial rocks?

My engineer friend formulated a clever method of making sure that he never fell foul to what he called 'financial predators' — that is, bills and outgoings that lurk in the undergrowth and pounce when you least expect it. Now, before we take another step, I must warn you that the engineer's method requires installation effort. If you're a lazy sod who subsists on handouts and free lunches, then you might want to pass this one up. Perhaps instead spend the time filling out lottery tickets or feeding the slots or daydreaming. But if, on the other hand, you're made of sterner stuff and you boast a determined disposition, read on for here's how to organise your accounts like an engineer.

The basic concept sees us assign each bill or annual outgoing with its own separate account. Once set-up and organised, and it is this stage that is most labour intensive, you are then to allocate a direct debit to filter small sums into each account (of course, you must ensure that the monthly instalments are correctly calculate so that they equal the total amount of the bill/outgoing). Over the year these small sums stack up eventually accumulating enough to cover the bill – if you're super savvy you'll set the amounts slightly higher so that a surplus builds. What's great about this method is that, when the accounts and direct debits are established, you literally never have to think about saving for a bill again. Basically, you've automated your finances so that computers, networks and that pitifully paid employee in New Delhi do the work for you! And what's more, online banking makes the process even easier.

Right, let's get down to brass tacks. Below I have created a flowchart that depicts how you might go about engineering your accounts so that whenever a yearly reminder drops on your doormat you've got the liquidity to cover it. (Please bear in mind that the flowchart is supposed to serve only as a representative insight; thus, the calculations and bill/outgoing amounts are purely fictitious.)

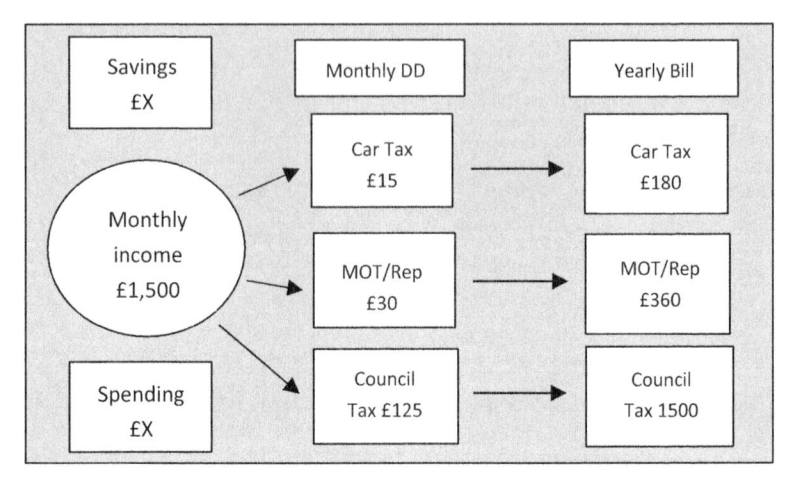

Savings £X	Monthly DD	Yearly Bill
	Car Tax £15	Car Tax £180
Monthly income £1,500	MOT/Rep £30	MOT/Rep £360
Spending £X	Council Tax £125	Council Tax 1500

I suppose, looking at that flowchart, which I must admit is quite busy, one could justifiably question the logic behind this system. After all, why not just pay the bills straight out of your current account? Why go through the hassle of setting up so many separate accounts? If you're scratching your head over these questions you've missed the point entirely. For many people, who perhaps aren't adept at saving or whose finances are in disarray, a single lump sum bill, such as the annual car tax or MOT, could result in living off smart price bread and beans for the next month. The implementation of this system could well be the difference between a state of semi-starvation or three wholesome squares a day.

The theory behind the engineer's method is that those small monthly direct debits sort of slip underneath the financial radar, to speak metaphorically. £15 here and £30 there aren't bank breaking outgoings; especially when they've been factored in to our monthly budget. But that surprise £360 MOT and essential repairs bill is liable to do to a poorly serviced account what that final strand of straw did to the camel's back. Snap! And what's more, when each bill has been accounted for and assigned its own direct debit, you know that the money left in your account afterwards is yours to do with as you please. I imagine for many this would offer much needed peace of mind.

The Joneses effect: just leave the bastards to it!

> But Keeping up with the Joneses is not cheap, and the costs go beyond dollars and cents. People work longer to afford what the competition requires, sacrificing time with their spouse or children. Divorce becomes more likely. Individuals may also take unwise financial risks to afford a more expensive lifestyle, increasing the likelihood of bankruptcy. And to afford a bigger

house, many choose to move father away from the expensive real estate near their jobs, resulting in punishingly long commutes and isolation from former friends, neighbours, and family members. All of these choices reduce individual and collective well-being.

The Wisest One in the Room – p. 191

Have you ever wondered while walking through a residential area why there's nearly always a cluster of houses sporting shiny new cars parked on the driveways? 'What's going on?' you might well ask. 'Have they all won the postcode lottery?' If you have ever noticed this strange social phenomenon, which expresses itself in many weird and wonderful ways, you may well be unwittingly witnessing the infamous 'keeping up with the Joneses' effect. 'The Joneses effect? What in the devil is that?' It's a curious psychological phenomenon that afflicts many millions of people worldwide. It goes by other names such as 'inferiority complex', 'copy-catism', 'insecurity', 'egocentricity' or 'I-can't-be-out-doneism'.

The way this psychological malady affects people is by making them feel worthless. These unpleasant feelings primarily manifest in the presence of a social contemporary who appears – on the surface – to be doing better financially and materially. The feelings can also be provoked by advertisements in magazines, social media and so on. The only way to assuage these feelings, so the sufferer erroneously believes, is to match like for like.

Of course, like popping a pill, the feelings of inferiority are only temporarily mitigated through the material acquisition. The 'high' that the purchase brings fades fast when Mr Jones appears on the scene with a new conspicuous consumable. A cure, as opposed to a quick fix, requires a significant psychological upgrade, which few people have the inclination, intelligence and technical expertise to bring about. Thus, it is better by far to study this neurological malady in others so that we may identify and immediately squash any burgeoning symptoms in ourselves and so avoid succumbing to what is certainly a most pathetic personality trait.

The financial and emotional havoc the Joneses effect can wreak is not to be taken lightly, despite my satirical tone, and you would be wise to take it quite seriously. Why? Well, for starters, incidences of people ruining themselves financially are all too numerous nowadays. As I write, a woman has been brought to trial and sentenced for a number of years in prison for defrauding banks out of huge sums so that she could support the illusion of being super wealthy. With borrowed money that she had no intention of paying back, she sustained a lavish lifestyle which enabled her to dine at the finest restaurants, take exotic holidays and pop over to Paris in a private jet for a shopping spree.

This, I concede, is an extreme example of the Joneses effect in action, and I would agree that few people afflicted with this condition con a bank out of £200,000 just so they can hire a Learjet to fly them to the fashion capital of the world. However, I'll stake an unused suppository on the supposition that there are hundreds of thousands of people throughout the land who, right now are running up dangerous levels of debt in a bid to present the external appearance of success. You might even be one of them and haven't realised it yet. But how would you know if you are rotten to the core with the Joneses effect? Because let's be honest here, few people who blow mounds of money on conspicuous material goods acknowledge that they are doing so to keep up appearances. Instead, they fuel their foolishness with falsities like 'I work hard, so why can't I have nice things?' or 'Well, Pete across the road's bought himself a shiny new penis extension. Why shouldn't I get one?'

The most obvious symptom of the Joneses effect is buying items that are socially esteemed – flashy cars, expensive watches, expensive handbags, coveted clothes brands, etc. Another symptom could be buying things that you just don't need. 'My pal Paul's gone and got himself a swish pair of sneaks – I should too!' Also, and perhaps this is the most ubiquitous symptom of the Joneses effect, following fashions. Why else would anyone change their wardrobe sixteen times a year (that's how many fashion 'seasons' there now are) other than to keep up with the Joneses?

If you can see shades of these symptoms in your buying behaviour, how might you go about curing yourself? For such a serious psychological malady I would normally recommend a frontal lobotomy. But I've just remembered the procedure's been banned. So a different tack is needed. Gilovich and Ross, authors of the book *The Wisest One in the Room* (see opening quote), recommend avoiding 'social comparisons that put you at the short end of the stick'. Certainly sound advice worth taking into consideration. After all, it is those comparisons that lead to self-denigrating thoughts and feelings of inferiority which are catalysts of consumerism. But avoiding social comparisons is nigh on impossible; unless, of course, you plan on becoming an agoraphobic or walking about with your eyes clamped shut.

No, avoiding social comparisons doesn't tackle the root of the problem. It's the equivalent of trying to cure a depressive disorder with a bottle of pills. The pills merely mask the problem – or offer temporary relief. We need a prophylactic. Here's one method which is almost guaranteed to work. On conclusion of this sentence, close the book, access the internet (or, better still, find a second-hand bookshop), search for a copy of Seneca's *Letters From A Stoic*, purchase a copy, and when it arrives read it – over and over and over again. Believe me, for a condition such as the Joneses effect (and living beyond your means) there is no pill more powerful or potent than the wisdom of Seneca.

> And how much do we acquire simply because our neighbours have acquired such things, or because most men possess them! Many of our troubles may be explained from the fact that we live according to a pattern, and, instead of arranging our lives according to reason, are led astray by convention.
>
> Seneca

Learn to be a bit more self-sufficient

A few years ago I was ordered by she-who-absolutely-must-be-obeyed to get the patio re-slabbed. That part of the garden, in all honesty, was an eyesore and needed some serious work. The slabs were like a mockery of a mosaic, all different colours, shapes and sizes, many cracked or broken, and in the middle stood the single most rickety shed in existence. However, as is usually the case with matters that concern building and construction, a woman is highly adept at identifying what needs to be done but entirely inept at comprehending the magnitude of the project.

So I politely and most humbly presented the argument to my other half that laying a new patio would require an awful lot of hard work, time and expertise – the latter of which I didn't readily possess. 'Poppycock!' was her immediate response. 'Just dig that bit up there,' she said, wagging her clueless finger, 'pop a couple of slabs in place and Bob's your uncle!'

As a compromise I suggested we phone a couple of landscaping contractors to come out and give us a quote. This move was calculated to strengthen my position. My thinking was that I would get the contractors to assess the job. They would support my contention that it is a substantial undertaking requiring significant expertise to execute. I could then use their professional analysis as a means of worming my way out of having to lift a finger. I naively expected them to quote around £1,000 – maybe £1,500 at most – which I would have happily paid if it got me out of digging dirt and mixing cement. But my dream of an easy life was dashed when both contractors quoted an eye-watering figure of £3,000.

That was a terrific sum of money just to remove a load of old slabs, dig out ten tons of topsoil (the area needed levelling), then fill in the space with a ton or two of aggregate, over which fifty shiny new slabs were to be laid. It was while expressing extreme disapproval at that price that an idea popped into my head. I could do much of the unskilled donkey work myself and pay the professionals to lay the slabs. Genius! So that's precisely what I did. I ordered two 8-ton skips and filled them to bursting. Then, after levelling off and preparing the space for the aggregate, I ordered two tons of said aggregate and made the 126 wheelbarrow trips needed to move it from point B (aka the end of my driveway) to point A (aka the big hole I'd made in the back garden).

Having prepared the foundations I called the contractors and asked them to come back and give me a second quote. When they arrived (on different days you understand) I was expecting not only some kudos for all my hard work, but also a significant reduction in price. I was somewhat perplexed when they came back to me with a price close to £2,800. After all that effort I'd saved a measly two hundred quid! Not on my wallet.

After banishing those knuckle-dragging, chain-smoking, Jack Daniels-swigging slack-jawed yokels from my garden I decided to do the sodding slabbing myself. Bollocks to it! I said. If I do a botched job and the slabs are a bit wonky and puddles form on rainy days, at least I'll have the satisfaction of being able to say: see that mess over there, I made that.

So that's exactly what I did. I ordered the slabs, sand, cement and mixer. I also persuaded my octogenarian father to lend an experienced eye (he adopted the role of quality control officer and provided instruction and advice on the 'levels' and 'viscosity of the mix'). In one morning, starting at 8.00 a.m. and finishing a little after 12 noon, I laid all fifty slabs and saved myself £2,000 (the materials and machinery cost twelve pounds shy of a grand) – which calculates out to an hourly wage of about £500!

That, I think you'll agree, is not a bad morning's savings.

All in all I did a pretty praiseworthy job that over the years has received a number of lofty compliments. And yes, puddles do form on rainy days.

How was I able to achieve this without any landscaping experience? Behold my secret: before I picked up a single slab I spent twenty minutes watching various slab-laying tutorials on YouTube. I find these online tutorials to be really very useful (I have also used YouTube self-help videos to teach myself how to unblock an outside drain, hang interior doors and play the guitar to a tolerable standard – those YouTube videos saved me literally thousands).

The moral of this tip is: when it comes to household jobs (and even to learning to play an instrument) consider giving it a go yourself before shelling out a king's ransom for a professional to pull your pants down. Chances are, unless it's something technical, such as fixing a faulty combi boiler or rewiring the electrics, you can probably do a half-decent job on your own.

Monetise: Verb (mʌn.ɪ.taɪz) 'to change something into money, to make money from something ...'

Right now, as you read these words, you might well be sitting on an oilfield of potential wealth. Yep, I'm being serious. Under your feet there could be a veritable reservoir of wealth waiting to be tapped. Okay, okay, stop fidgeting in excitement and looking down at the floor. You're not going to see it unless you get up off your arse, go find a mirror and marvel at your potentially lucrative reflection. Let me ask a quick question: do you have a hobby, talent, interest and/or specialist knowledge?

Now, if the answer to the question is a resounding *no* – 'No, I'm a sad git who doesn't have a hobby' or 'No, I'm a boring fart who doesn't have any interests' – feel free to skip to the next point. If, however, you answered *yes* – 'Yes, I do have a hobby!' or 'Yes, I do possess specialist knowledge!' – read on because you could be missing out on an opportunity to monetise that hobby or specialist knowledge. Let me give you a few examples to illustrate what I mean. All names, for the sake of confidentiality, are faux – but the cases are credible.

Susie spent her evenings making jewellery, earrings, necklaces, bracelets and brooches. This she did because – well, she possessed a natural artistic inclination that needed an outlet and it provided her with marginally more pleasure than the TV. She never considered selling her jewellery for the simple reason that she believed them to possess no commercial value; it was merely a hobby, and you can't make money from a hobby, or so she thought. That changed one evening when at a social event a friend complimented her on a matching necklace and earring set she happened to be wearing and asked where she'd purchased them. When Susie said that she had personally designed and created the shiny trinkets herself, her friend placed an order on the spot. It didn't take long for news to spread and before she knew it Susie had a small client base. Susie now runs a sideline business that provides her with a secondary income.

A year into retirement Tim wasn't enjoying the high life as much as he thought he would. Not only was his pension worth considerably less than he envisioned but he was struggling to fill the 'endless hollow' hours. However, he didn't want to clamp on the employment shackles again either; after thirty years of working he had had more than his fill of kowtowing to the arbitrary whims of middle management and struggling to meet unachievable deadlines. Thus his conundrum, as he saw it, was twofold: (1) how to supplement his measly pension (preferably with cash-in-hand work); and (2) how to occupy his leisure time. The problem was, Tim had not cultivated a talent, skill or specialist knowledge that he could monetise. However, he was a dog lover and regularly looked after his son's pet pooch, Pepper. With a little encouragement from his son, Tim put a small advert in the local paper advertising a dog-sitting service. While running the advert he applied for a boarding permit from the local council. Within a matter of weeks he received a number of bookings – mainly daytime sitters at first. But after the owners got to know Tim they felt comfortable leaving their dogs with him while they went on vacation. A year on from advertising in the paper, Tim's doggy day care service, as he jokingly called it, was bringing in more money (tax-free) than his pension and it provided him with a purpose and pleasant pastime.

Gary and his wife Julie are both keen triathletes. They're not professionals, just passionate amateurs who love the sport. It was this love that compelled Gary (with the support of Julie) to organise a local training club – pro bono. What, for free! Yep, firstly he started working with would-be triathletes, helping them prepare for up-and-coming events and competitions. He didn't stop there though. Once he'd built up a bit of a following he organised his very own triathlon event – only a sprint distance at first. Because they're short-duration events that tend to last no longer than a couple of hours, Gary used this to test the waters. When it went off without a hitch he felt emboldened enough to organise a couple more until the season closed. The following year, after a string of successful events, he had a bash at a half Ironman. Organising an event of this magnitude – 1.5-mile swim, 56-mile cycle, 13.2-mile run – required commitment and the coordination of multiple moving parts. But at nearly £100 per entry the financial rewards were significant. On the day over 350 athletes competed. The event was a great success (to which I can personally attest as I was one of the sadists who took part). Gary now runs one major and four minor events every year – as well as his free training clubs.

My final example is a personal one. My one and only vice is overindulging an inveterate predilection for literature, learning and knowledge (kind of the same thing really). Over the years I've amassed a sizeable and ever-growing corpus of books – in excess of 1,500. Now, I don't make mention of this to impress you – 'Check me out, I've got a shitload of books. That must mean I'm a real smart-arse!' – that is not the case. I make mention of my incurable addiction because in partnership with my significant other I developed it into a small sideline business. One day – literally, one random run-of-the-mill day – we decided to open an online store through which we would hawk our surplus of books.

Now, unlike that pestilential infestation of entrepreneurs that plague YouTube, I'm not going to lie and say that setting up the store or running an online business was a walk in the park and that within a week we were making a killing. The truth of it was that setting up an online store required time, effort and Teflon patience – the bureaucratic and administrative hoops you must leap through will test your sanity. Also, when you've finally created your eStore and come up with a catchy name (ours is *Bountiful Bazaar* – corny, I know, but all the good names had gone), you then have to tackle the Herculean labour of 'uploading' your inventory. If that's 500 books it takes a while. However, at the end of one day of uploading books we managed to create a hundred-strong inventory which amounted to £1,000 in stock.[3]

I'll be straight with you, the online store was nothing more than an experiment and I harboured no hope of moving our merchandise. But amazingly, within twelve hours of going live – after waiting nearly nine days for some miniscule cog in the enormous Amazon machine to push a button that would grant us access to the greatest marketplace the world has ever seen – we'd sold two books. Before the end of the first day we'd sold

---

[3] If you ever decide to embark on a venture such as creating an online store, know before you do that everyone is on the take and the further down the pecking order you reside the more that will be taken from you. Here's what I mean. I remember after uploading those first hundred books my other half rubbing her hands together at the prospect of making a £1,000 profit. I also remember the displeasure of having to bring her attention to the myriad leeches that would suck up at least 25% of our profits long before it found its way to our pockets. Also, we'd be lucky if we sold half of our inventory. There aren't many people willing to part with £100 for an antiquarian folio containing a collection of the writings of Galileo. Some of the books would probably never sell. That's not just the case for books but for *all* commodities. I advise before undertaking any venture to do your research first and uncover all the hidden costs, fees and expenses. The platform provider – in this case eBay/Amazon – deduct a percentage of the end sale price for using their platform. Then there might be a 'closing' fee (Amazon charges between £0.50 and £0.95 to close each successful sale). In addition, depending on where your merchandise is stored, you may have to pay for storage. Then there's postage (yes, customers are usually charged for postage, but if it is miscalculated, or the item is returned, then it is you who picks up the bill). Then there are debit/credit card transaction fees. Don't forget to include paying yourself a wage for the time invested in uploading to the platform and going to the post office. There might also be marketing fees, and, of course, if the item is returned you've not only lost the sale but incurred all the other fees. I'm not trying to put you off, just making sure you're informed.

five! And in a week over 10% of our inventory had been bought. Beggars belief!

Become an e-com king (or queen)

'An e-com king? What in the hell's one of those?' You don't know? Have a guess. 'Is it the medical term for a person who's addicted to pornography?' Not quite. Irrespective of whether or not you've heard of an e-com king before, I can almost guarantee that at some point in the past year (probably in the past week) you will have come into contact with one and maybe even donated a few pounds to their coffers.

An e-com king (or queen) is merely an honorary title bestowed upon those who make it big in the seedy world of e-commerce, that is: electric or internet commerce. The e-commer is little more than a middleman/woman who looks to mediate the exchange of goods (usually pointless plastic products) for money between manufacturers and consumers.

You – yes, you – the one holding this book – even you could be crowned an e-com king/queen. Me? I hear you exclaim, heart palpitating as you quiver with excitement at the thought of making it BIG!

Anyone can join the ever-expanding ranks of parasites that are making money exploiting the two most abundant resources in human society, namely poverty and ignorance. It's a reverse Robin Hood scheme where, instead of stealing from the rich to give to the poor, you're exploiting the poor and selling to the rich (and the poor). And this is how you do it in seven super-duper easy-peasy lemon squeezy simple steps:

(1) Decide what you want to sell – clothes, plastics, accessories for pets are very popular at the moment. It could be kidneys, babies – whatever it is, just decide.

(2) Open a 'shop' (inverted commas to denote condescension; most online shops are mirages). You can open your shop on Amazon, eBay or Shopify. There is a veritable panoply of platform providers to choose from.

(3) Open an account with Ali Express, the Chinese version of Amazon. (This is where the exploitation of poverty begins. Thus it is important at this step to dispense with morality – remember: morality and moneymaking are mutually exclusive; or, as the prince of palaeontology, Stephen Jay Gould, would put it, non-overlapping magisteria.)

(4) 'Import' (more condescension-denoting commas, for you don't import a damn thing. This is drop-shipping – no upfront costs involved) ... import into your store the images and descriptions of the products you wish to hawk.

(5) Hike the prices. (This is where we begin exploiting the ignorant).

(6) Open a business page on a social media platform – preferably Facebook because, by all accounts, that's where the most ignorant members of our species hang out. Then advertise the shit out of your product. Seriously, you need to launch a Nazi-style propaganda campaign and indoctrinate as many of those ignorant social media types as possible: if they're not asphyxiating on your ads you ain't doing it right!

184

(7) Kick back, relax and wait for the coin to come rolling in.

So, in seven super simple steps (six really: kicking back and relaxing doesn't constitute as a step), you could be the proud owner of an e-commerce drop-shipping business. And if you choose to follow those seven steps you stand to make a pretty penny. I'm sure the naive or innocent among you will be scratching your heads wondering how you can make money like that. By exploiting the poor and the ignorant, remember!

Let me explain. China is packed to bursting with two things: poverty and people. For the e-com king wannabe this is a veritable gold mine waiting to be exploited (actually it's been mercilessly exploited for the past twenty years, so hurry!). You see, about 98% of all Chinese people are stuck in a miserable state of economic servitude, meaning that if they don't work, they'll starve to death. Again, perfect for the e-com king. Why? Well, all those poor desperate souls will willingly work in Dickensian-style factories for eighteen-plus hours a day for a cup of water and a pot to piss into an hour later. What's the consequence of this? An abundance of mega-cheap crap that can be sold to blind ignorant Westerners.

And what's truly marvellous about this set-up is that the e-com king doesn't need to run the risk of buying products upfront and storing them in a warehouse. How? By using drop-shipping to fulfil orders. The e-com king is little more than an illusory link in a long chain that stretches from East to West. They present the image of legitimacy to the ignorant while selling sweatshop-made products at over ten times their manufacturing cost. Yep, you read that right – ten times the cost of production!

'How do you know all this?' How? Because I've dabbled in e-coming before, that's how. Don't you dare look at me with those judgemental eyes. Yeah, I'm not going to deny it, it's immoral. Yeah, I concede, it's exploitative. Yeah, I won't argue, we e-commers are screwing *everyone* over. But if we don't do it, somebody else will. They don't call this capitalism for nothing you know!

Five-star fallacy
☆ ☆ ☆ ☆ ☆

The one positive of pursuing the e-com king crown is that even if you fail, and you almost certainly will, you'll get a glimpse behind the capitalist curtain. Seated in the theatre all you see is the show, with its dazzling lights and practiced actors who dance through the obfuscating smoke and mirrors. But this is all a hideous illusion devised to blind you from the reality of contemporary consumerism. It is an attempt to blur the bullshit. One peek behind the curtain and you'll see how the capitalists are literally robbing you in broad daylight – not only robbing you but, worse in my opinion, *manipulating* you.

This is nothing new. In the 1950s Vance Packard pointed out in the opening pages of his book, *The Hidden Persuaders*, that 'many of us are being influenced and manipulated – far more than we realise – in the patterns of our everyday lives. Large-scale efforts,' he goes on, 'are being made, often with impressive success, to channel our unthinking habits, our purchasing decisions, and our thought processes by the use of insights gleaned from psychiatry and the social sciences.'[4]

Take the star rating, for example, which bamboozles consumers into believing that a product is better than it really is. Today, reviews, customer feedback, and star ratings are the be-all and end-all of the contemporary business model, and capitalists have cottoned on to our herd-like mentality. Humans, as it happens, are more like sheep than they care to admit.

If your product has only a few – or, god forbid, no – reviews you will struggle to sell. Bad reviews are even worse; they can kill a product altogether or seriously slow sales. You know what they say about one or two bad apples – they'll spoil an entire cartload. The importance of customer reviews explains why companies wage review wars. It's not uncommon for a company to deposit into the cart of a competitor a number of mouldy reviews.

However, the conundrum this presents to the aspiring e-com king is how to get good reviews and stacks of ratings when first starting out. This was a hurdle that I believed to be insurmountable. When I launched an e-commerce company I couldn't help covet the immense ratings of my competitors. How the hell have they got over a thousand 5-star reviews? I often asked with great perplexity. The enigma was resolved when my business partner serendipitously stumbled upon an app that, for a little less than £10, enabled you to 'import'

---

[4] V. Packard, *The Hidden Persuaders*. London: Penguin (1957).

reviews for your product. You could literally access a huge database of reviews and cherry-pick which ones you wanted.

Welcome, Messieurs-dames, to what I call the five-star fallacy, and once you're aware of it you'll never trust a review again.

A couple of ethical questions remain. For example:

Q: How many of the customer reviews imported are genuine? I was able to create multiple fake reviews. In fact, on Shopify the proprietor can just pen their own – pictures and all. I couldn't be bothered to write my own so I copied and pasted reviews straight from Amazon.

Q: Do the people who feature in these reviews know that they have been monetised and converted into a tradable commodity? I'd be gobsmacked if they did ... that's if they're genuine (and you get the feeling that many aren't).

Other morally suspect practices that you might feel compelled to engage in, if you wish one day to wear that e-com crown, include the tremendous hike in prices and exploitation of Third-World manufacturers. Whenever some faceless consumer purchased a product from my store, which would prompt my phone to notify me with a 'Ch-Ching!' ringtone (I became conditioned to that ringtone. Every time it 'Ch-Chinged!' I'd salivate uncontrollably like one of Pavlov's dogs and see shimmering pound signs slowly spin before my eyes), I couldn't help but think 'Moron! Haaa! You've just had your pants pulled down! That plastic novelty bust of Prince Charles cost a tenth of what you've just paid me! *Id-ee-ut. Id-ee-ut!*'

I know it's horrible to chastise customers but, well, they deserve it. Why? For buying sweatshop-made tack at a hundred times the manufacturing cost – tack, no doubt, that they don't need.

All kidding aside e-comming is not quite the Sunday morning lazy lie-in I've portrayed it to be. I suppose I was just having a dig at those irritating parasites that pop up on YouTube adverts peddling mistruths and falsities. Just the other day one told me that I could make £10,000 a month by selling online. But not before first making me feel inferior by flashing his enormous earnings. Five whole seconds I had to endure this verminous weasel wax lyrical about how I could, after a couple of clicks, be living the 'laptop lifestyle' when all I wanted to do was watch cats act like prats.

The truth of it is, if you want to succeed in e-commerce, or affiliate marketing, or anything where there's money to be made, you have to be prepared to invest a shit-ton of time and money. When I first set up my 'store', I worked eighteen-hour days for a week. I then poured buckets of pennies into the pocket of the third richest man in the world for the privilege of advertising my products. For weeks all I incurred was expense. That, my friends, is the reality of it. As the saying goes, there's no such thing as a free lunch. And all this is becoming increasingly difficult because more and more people are fighting for a place at the buffet table. Truly, the contemporary e-commer is like one of those parasite-ridden club-footed city pigeons hobbling about pecking at the crumbs dropped by passers-by. But there's still bread enough to go around – for a limited time only!

* * *

What I've endeavoured to do with these Treasure Trove tips is demonstrate the unlikely places where wealth can dwell. With a bit of imagination and a small initial investment (though it didn't cost Tim a penny to get his dog-sitting business off the ground), I am confident that most people could create a consistent secondary income without having to pull an evening shift at the local convenience store or endure some other species of drudgery. By exercising a bit of imagination and thinking about how that hobby or interest could be monetised, you might bring home a few extra slices of bacon doing something you enjoy.

Tip 9: The Death Pledge (aka the mortgage)

The Mortgager and Mortgagee differ, the one from the other, not more in length of purse than the jester and jestee do in that of memory. But in this the comparison between them runs, as the scholiasts call it, upon all-four; – which, by the bye, is upon one or two legs more than some of the best of Homer's can pretend to; – namely, That the one raises a sum, and the other a laugh, at your expense, and thinks no more about it. Interest, however, still runs on in both cases; – the periodical or accidental payments of it just serving to keep the memory of the affair alive; till, at length, in some evil hour – pop comes the creditor upon each, and by demanding principal upon the spot, together with full interest to the very day, makes them both feel the full extent of their obligations.

Laurence Sterne
The Life and Opinions of Tristram Shandy

I've dropped the M-bomb many times before now but only in passing. Up to this point, mortgages have been mentioned as a means of illustrating a point or to buttress a weak argument. But considering that a mortgage places by far the greatest financial burden on the average person's back – it is usually the biggest ball we drag about – I thought it prudent to give it a place of prominence in this book on money-saving ideas. This tip will not merely advise the reader on how their mortgage can be reduced and why it is imperative that we pay more than the capital repayments (though these topics will, of course, be discussed), it will also delineate the various mortgage products available while providing the prospective first-time buyer with an overview of the different routes to making the death pledge. The reader who is already in bondage to a usurious lender might well want to skip ahead to 'Why we should make additional capital repayments on our mortgage' and 'How to make additional mortgage repayments'. The reader who is about to climb onto the property ladder should read it all from beginning to end.

What is a mortgage?

The word 'mortgage' derives from the Old French words *mort* meaning 'dead' and *gage* meaning 'pledge' – literally 'dead pledge'. It is only fitting that such a morbid term should become the name of the contract which is very nearly the equivalent of signing your life away. Make of that what you will.

According to Google Dictionary, a mortgage is 'a legal agreement by which a bank, building society, etc. lends money *at interest* in exchange for taking title of the debtor's property, with the condition that the conveyance of title becomes void upon the payment of the debt.'

Put another way. You want that house, but you can't afford the six-figure price tag that comes with it. But you want it nonetheless. So, in desperation, you turn to a bank to see if they'd be willing to buy the house on your behalf. They would be willing. The bank agrees to take on the loan so long as you agree to take on their interest rates and terms and conditions. You are willing. Now, for the next 20-plus years, you must faithfully and consistently give the bank a sizeable portion of your monthly income.

How it works (in reality)
I wonder how the average home 'owner' would explain how a mortgage works. It is my contention that, if asked, the majority of people who pay a mortgage would firstly frown, then stutter through an ambiguous explanation: 'Well, it's like … you know … where the bank like … lends you some of their money … like … so you can own a home … or something.' From the soft well-indented seat of superiority I smile patronisingly at their childlike naivety. 'Oh how pitifully naive they are,' I can't help but think as I twirl the frayed ends of my moustache and puff on my pipe. But then my face is wiped clean of that condescending smirk when I remember that that's precisely how I would have answered the question for the first ten years of my mortgage-paying career. Unless you're willing to take the time and go to the trouble to find out, you'll forever remain behind that pleasant veil of ignorance.

It isn't nice to learn that the bank that has fastened a financial ball and chain around your ankle for the next twenty-five years can only do so because the government has bequeathed it that power. Also, it's rather depressing to know that for every fictitious pound the bank lends you, you'll most likely have to pay two real ones back. However, although these realisations are apt to induce deep depression, we can direct those negative emotions to drive positive behaviour, behaviour that can bring about an early termination of the death pledge.

So here's how a mortgage works: firstly, a price is agreed between the purchaser and the seller of a property. Let's say the price of the property is £200,000, which in London would get you a Portaloo and in Wales a country estate. The borrower, who we'll assume has a minimum deposit of 10% (so £20,000), solicits the services of a mortgage broker whose job it now is to hunt down the best mortgage deal. The broker quickly locates a lender and as long as the borrower meets their stringent application criteria (do they have a pulse?), they will fasten a cuff around the borrower's ankle for the life of the mortgage. Usually when the lender agrees to take on the mortgage nothing much happens for a considerable period of time; sometimes many weeks or months may pass without the slightest hint that anything is being done. This is possibly because the lender wants the borrower to believe that the process is a highly complex one, that even in this technological age of ours it's no mean feat to move about sizeable sums of money. Which is complete poppycock, of course.

Once the funds for the mortgage have been fabricated out of the ether, something strange and mysterious happens. Interest is added on. Depending on the length of the mortgage – five years, ten years, twenty-five years – and the interest rate – 2%, 3%, 4%, 5% – that original £180,000 (minus the £20,000 deposit, remember) could more than double. And there we have the

Seventh Wonder of the financial world: money made from nothing!

Different types of mortgage products
Really there are five types of mortgage available to us:

- (1) the mortgage of Mum and Dad;
- (2) capital repayment;
- (3) interest-only;
- (4) buy-to-let; and
- (5) shared equity/partnership.

Each mortgage type serves a different function and has its own idiosyncratic characteristics. So let's look at each of them in more detail.

(1) The mortgage of Mum and Dad
This is arguably the best option out of a bad bunch and it works like this: your mum and dad pay the mortgage while you, leech that you are, live under their roof rent-free. If your conscience gets the better of you, you can make a token monthly donation towards your keep. When your mum and dad shuffle off their mortal coil, you get a free house! This is the one and only positive of this type of mortgage. There are many negatives.

For starters, you'll have to live in close proximity with your parents, perhaps for a considerable length of time, until they pop their clogs. I don't know about you, but even the promise of a free home could not induce me to live with my parents. Another downside is that they will expect to be cared for when they eventually grow old and decrepit or become senile. This job will inevitably fall to you – that's if you don't want to see the house you've been so patiently waiting for left to a cattery in their will. When you own your own home, or at least lease one off the bank for the best years of your life, you are effectively emancipated from such a lamentable duty and can instead sling the Aged Parents in a care home.

(2) Capital repayment mortgage

For the vast majority of borrowers this is really the only viable option – that is, if you plan to own your home one day. A capital repayment mortgage works as follows: when you make monthly payments, a slice finds its way into the bank's coffers through interest deductions and what's leftover goes to reducing the capital balance. To illustrate this legalised robbery I've created a flowchart:

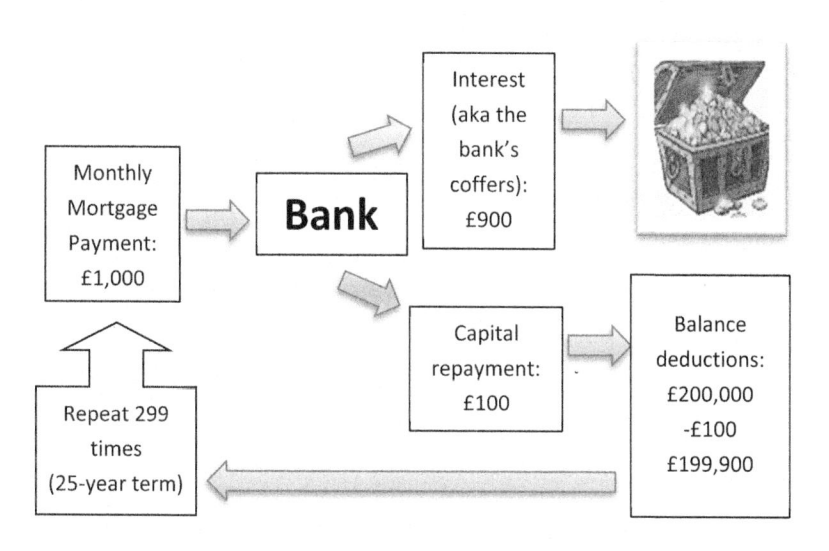

```
Monthly Mortgage Payment: £1,000  →  Bank  →  Interest (aka the bank's coffers): £900

                                          →  Capital repayment: £100  →  Balance deductions:
                                                                         £200,000
                                                                         -£100
                                                                         £199,900

Repeat 299 times (25-year term)  ←
```

Of course, over time, when the term or the mortgage reduces, the monthly payments will not remain so miserably asymmetrical and a greater portion of each payment will go to reducing the capital balance.

The obvious positive of the capital repayment option is that, sometime in the distant future, as long as you continue to make your monthly payments and resist the temptation to release equity, you will sever the fetters and find yourself liberated from financial servitude. For some unknown reason it has become quite the fashion, especially among retirees, to borrow more money from the bank, thus extending their mortgage or starting an entirely new one.

People release equity for a number of reasons, few of them are very smart. These reasons include, for example, financing a world cruise, living the high life for a month or two, making 'home improvements'. Unless you are looking to invest the money, the aim of which would be to bring a greater return than the interest you are now paying on it, it is almost never a good idea to release equity. All you'll be doing is paying extra on whatever it is you plan to spend the money on. (Few people factor this in to their decision-making: when you pay for that world cruise with borrowed money you are, effectively, having your pants pulled down twice; the first time by paying over the odds for the cruise and the second time by paying interest to the bank.)

You also need to consider two main types of repayment mortgage: one with a variable interest rate and one where the interest rate is fixed over time.

Variable interest rate

With a variable mortgage the interest rate fluctuates as and when the boys at the Bank of England deem it necessary to turn the base rate knob up or down. One benefit of taking out a variable mortgage is that the interest rate is usually a percentage or two lower than a fixed-rate mortgage. However, the main drawback is the instability factor. You must know that when selecting a variable mortgage your monthly payments may rise and fall in response to the base interest rate. Now, the Bank of England can only raise the national interest rate by 0.25% every six months. So if you were flirting with the variable mortgage, it wouldn't be the case that you'd wake up one morning to be greeted with the news that the interest rate had jumped to 15%. However, in saying that, even a 0.25% interest hike could translate to a noticeable increase in your monthly payments.

Fixed interest rate

Here, the lender would lock the borrower in to a mortgage contract for a fixed-term – say, two, three or five years – at a fixed interest rate – say, 2.5%, 3%, 4%. How it normally works is that the longer the term, the higher the interest rate. Of course, by fixing the borrower into a term of, say, five years, the bank is kind of taking a risk, because if interest rates were to rise – if the boys at the Bank of England were playing with their knobs again – the lender would have lost out on an opportunity to screw the borrower out of more money. That's why the interest rate on a fixed-term is usually a couple of per cent higher. The positive of the fixed-rate is the stability element. To fix in for two, three or five years means that for two, three or five years your interest rate will not go up (or down), thus your monthly payments will remain stable. Some sleep better knowing that.

A word of warning with the fixed-rate mortgage. Prior to agreeing to a fixed-term, which will contractually nail you to a repayment cross for between two to five years, it might be wise to spend an hour or two researching economic forecasts and checking the Bank of England's future fiscal agenda. Why? Because they could both impact on the base interest rate, which in turn could make fixing a mortgage rate either a good or a bad idea. Here's an example to illustrate this point.

The year before the financial crash of 2008 thousands of people fixed into a mortgage with an interest rate between 3.5% and 5.5%. After the crash, the Bank of England dropped the base rate to less than 1% in an attempt to reduce the burden on borrowers. For those unfortunate souls still stuck on an interest rate of, say, 4%, their monthly payments would have been much higher than if they had waited.

If you had a mortgage of £100,000 over twenty-five years at a rate of 4%, your monthly payments would work out at a little over £525. The same mortgage over the same time at a rate of 1% reduces the monthly payments to £370.[5] That's a reduction of a whopping £155 a month, or £1,860 a year. Borrowers who fixed at 4% for five years prior to the 2008 crash would have begrudgingly paid an additional £9,300 over the term!

---

[5] As I write, in May 2020, the base rate is an unbelievable 0.1%.

So what's best – a fixed-rate mortgage or a variable-rate mortgage? Ultimately only you can answer that question; the responsibility of making that decision should never be annexed to a second party such as a financial advisor. That's precisely the mistake I made toward the back end of 2007. Because I couldn't be bothered to do the intellectual legwork myself when weighing up the pros and cons of the variable and fixed-rate mortgage, I followed the advice of a broker and fixed for five years at an interest rate of 4.5%. Two months later – crash! A bunch of greedy bankers drove the Western world's economy over a cliff. Shortly afterwards, interest rates fell, and fell, and continued to fall, eventually setting new historical lows. This cautionary tale should act as a warning. Learn from this fool and do your own decision-making. That way you'll only have yourself to blame.

(3) Interest-only mortgage

This is where you essentially rent the property from the bank – you become the bank's tenant. Yeah, no thanks! An interest-only mortgage is exactly that: the borrower borrows from the bank the capital to acquire the property but then only repays the interest. The principal – the amount borrowed – will never decrease, thus the lender will never own the property. This is analogous to running on a treadmill: you've got to sweat and suffer just to stay stationary.

Those readers with their heads screwed on the right way round might well be wondering: 'Who in god's good name would make interest-only payments? Surely you'd have to be either a complete idiot or raving lunatic?' It is a curiosity, I must admit.

But, you might be surprised to learn, there are some sensible reasons for choosing this option.

For example, if someone is going through a rough patch they could, by transitioning from capital repayments to interest-only, significantly reduce the size of their monthly mortgage contribution, which could make the difference between keeping or losing their home. In a sorry situation such as this, where needs must, switching to interest-only might be an expedient option. However, you would be unwise to make interest-only payments on your primary property for any more than a year – two at max. If your financial affairs have failed to improve during that time, the better option would be to sell up, buy a cheaper property and transition back to a capital repayment mortgage.

The inveterate house-hopper who's looking to exploit a rise in property prices might decide, for the short time they plan to dwell in their non-fixed abode, to keep expenses low and pay only the interest.

If you want to acquire a property to rent and plan to use the tenant's payments as a supplementary income, then interest-only could well be the sensible option. But if you one day want to own the roof that keeps the rain off your head, capital repayment is a must.

(4) Buy-to-let
The one mortgage that could make you money! Buy-to-let is an investment venture and one that has made a small number of people extremely wealthy and a large number of people

moderately financially comfortable. I know several people who have second, third and fourth homes that they rent and I can't help but feel a little envious at the nice nest egg they're building. Of all the investment options available to us – stocks and shares/venture capital/ISA – buy-to-let is arguably one of the safest.

By acquiring a second property to let you have a number of options of wealth augmentation at your disposal. I will consider three.

The first option, then, is to use the tenant's payments as a secondary or supplementary income. But do remember to take into account the myriad leeches that will start to suck the blood from this income. For example, you'll have to:

- pay a tax contribution on secondary earnings;
- pay interest on the capital of the property (obviously);
- put some aside each month in case the boiler breaks or the sink springs a leak or the tenant decides to go Johnny Cash on your property;
- pay a letting agent to do the job that you can't be bothered to do; and
- pay a form of insurance for letters.

The £600 you envisaged you'd make each month off your shiny new buy-to-let property could shrink to as low as £200. Still, £2,400 a year is not to be sniffed at. It's for this reason buy-to-lets are better long-term investments. For unless you pay off a sizeable chunk of the principal, thus bringing mortgage payments down, little will be leftover for you. And failure to reinvest 'earnings' back into the property could result in calamity.

If you take out an interest-only mortgage to secure your buy-to-let property, with the view of supplementing your income, be aware that, like all investment ventures, it comes with an element of risk.

For example, let's say house prices were slowly creeping up when you acquired your buy-to-let property, and during this inflationary boon you were enjoying the extra income. But then house prices suddenly and unexpectedly take a nosedive. This could leave you in the unpalatable position of owning a second home that's now in negative equity. Here's how you could find yourself in negative equity through a buy-to-let venture:

(1) Enter the market when house prices are high or climbing.
(2) Acquire a buy-to-let property for £150,000.
(3) Land a tenant and charge them at least three times the interest repayment.
(4) Spend what's leftover of the tenant's payments, not thinking to reinvest it back into the property.
(5) House prices suddenly and unexpectedly take a nosedive.
(6) A slimy estate agent values your house at £125,000 – that's if you could even sell it.
(7) Have a little cry.
(8) Your buy-to-let property has depreciated by 16.6% of its original value, but you still owe the bank the full

£150,000! You are now in a deep hole of negative equity that could take years to climb out of.

(9) This leaves you with three options:
(i) Sell and swallow the substantial loss (you'd be an idiot to do this).
(ii) Hold on to the property and do your best to keep it occupied but stop spunking the tenant's payments up the wall.
(iii) Burn it to the ground, preferably when the tenant is out, and claim off the insurance (make sure you have insurance before taking this option).

A second approach to buy-to-let, and this is probably the most common, is that of cultivating a long-term investment. To stand any chance of achieving this goal you must dispense with any hopes of short-term profiteering or generating a secondary income. Instead, you would invest 100% of the profit back into the property with a view to clearing the capital as quickly as possible. By taking this route you could, when you reach retirement, have a second property bought and paid for, giving you the option of either letting or liquidating.

The third buy-to-let approach is to try to time your purchase to take advantage of changing economic circumstances which can, if you get it right, substantially swell the price of your property. (When I moved for the second time property prices climbed precipitously and in little over a year the value of my house had increased by £68,000. I hasten to add that this pecuniary boon was pure luck.) However, though potentially very lucrative, few possess the requisite economic forecasting acumen or psychological resolve to see it through to fruition.

(5) Shared equity/partnership mortgage
The shared equity/partnership mortgage is a joint venture where the borrower seeks an additional loan through a second-party lender to help finance a mortgage that they perhaps otherwise wouldn't be able to secure. The theory behind the shared equity mortgage is that the second-party lender – which could be a building firm, a local authority or a government help-to-buy scheme, for example – is entitled to a percentage of the equity that the house accrues when it is resold.

However, with a shared equity loan, as with a partnership mortgage, the borrower still has to pay their primary mortgage as well as the equity loan and/or second-party partner. It's for this reason that I have absolutely no understanding of precisely how this is supposed to help first-time buyers climb onto the property ladder. From researching the shared equity/partnership mortgage it appears that the second-party loan is, in some instances, put forward to help bring the monthly repayments down so they are within the borrower's means. The second-part loan is suspended for a period of time – that is, for two to five years, the borrower only has to pay back the reduced-sized mortgage to the primary lender. Is this getting confusing yet?

Let's have a look at a simplified step-by-step process to see if we can clear the fog of confusion.

Single lender capital repayment route
    (1) Purchase property for £200,000.
    (2) Put down a deposit of 20% – (£40,000).

(3) After deposit, borrow £160,000 from primary lender. Mortgage term is 30 years; interest rate is 3%.
(4) Monthly repayments would be around £675.

Shared equity/partnership route
(1) Purchase property for £200,000.
(2) Put down a deposit of 20% – (£40,000).
(3) Shared equity/partnership mortgage loan (10-year term) matches the initial deposit – (£40,000).
(4) After deposit and shared equity loan deductions, borrow £120,000 from primary lender. Mortgage term is 30 years; interest rate is 3%.
(5) Monthly mortgage repayments to primary lender would be around £500.

As you can see, on comparing and contrasting the two methods, through the shared equity/partnership route the monthly mortgage repayments are reduced by around 25%. But, I have to ask, at what cost? The second-party lender is going to want their slice of the pie sooner or later. Last year I read a disconcerting report in a reputable national paper (so not the *Daily Star*, *The Sun* or *Daily Mirror*) that exposed how many building firms are exploiting the government help-to-buy scheme by inflating the price of new properties. They can do this because the secondary lender is reducing the primary mortgage load. This then lulls the (usually naive) first-time buyer into the false belief that they can 'afford' a house above what their wages would normally permit

---

Rule 1 for [...] homeowners is never ever borrow more than you can pay back. Excessive debt hurts all people.

William J. O'Neil.

and that the house will be worth considerably more than when they initially acquired it. But the newspaper report showed that the complete opposite was in fact happening. The first-time buyer, thanks to the secondary loan, could afford to secure a mortgage above their earnings only because for the first two to five years they don't have to pay back the secondary loan. But when this secondary loan kicks in, increasing the monthly repayments by as much as 25%, it can place an intolerable burden on the borrower. Also, because the original house price was inflated, when the house is put back on the market, many first-time buyers discover that they have little to no equity in the property.

My advice to anyone considering the shared equity/partnership mortgage is: don't. I would suggest that you set your sights lower and seek a moderate property, one that is commensurate with your annual income.

The first house I took a mortgage out on was a poky little one-bedroom maisonette that cost £85,500. The monthly repayments were a paltry £350, which enabled me to enjoy a reasonable standard of living while keeping the rain off my back. I'm of the firm belief that at most your mortgage should never exceed more than five times your earnings. But three times is optimal. This way, if interest rates rose or you suffered a financial setback, you could comfortably absorb these pecuniary impacts.

The problem today is that too many people want to live in a big fancy house even if that means saddling themselves with a debt that in reality they can't support. This is called living beyond your means (see **Rule 10: Live Within Your Means**). Millions of homeowners are overextended because their huge mortgages eat up a substantial portion of their monthly income leaving little remaining. If your mortgage is gobbling up seventy or more per cent of your monthly earnings, then you are one of those millions and you've placed yourself in a precarious financial position. At a time when interest rates have hit rock bottom this illusion might be sustainable. But when those interest rates creep back up, and they will (if economic history is anything to go by), that 70% could climb to 80, 90 or 100% of earnings. (My mum loves telling me the story of when she bought her first house in the seventies just as the interest rates climbed to a whopping 15%. If that happened today, it'd be 2008 all over again.) On the run up to the sub-prime mortgage cataclysm, the rise in interest rates pushed the repayments of some mortgages above 100% of earnings – above! Imagine that, your mortgage payments costing more than you earn!

Why you should make additional capital repayments on your mortgage

It goes something like this. You (or your broker) search out a mortgage lender who can offer you the term and interest rate that, together, will bring your dream house into your financial sphere. Great! The mortgage offer arrives in the post, you promptly sign it and send it back, including, of course, your account details. A few months later the lender starts sucking a sizeable chunk of your earnings out of your account. Not so great. At this point, like the vast majority of borrowers, you'll forget about your mortgage and you won't think about it until the fixed-term expires. At which point you might decide to renew with the same lender or look for one offering a slightly lower interest rate.

Then you'll carry on forgetting about it. This is the number one mistake most borrowers make. But why is it a mistake?

In the Financial Strategy section of this book, I explained how I hewed a colossal £35,000 off my mortgage merely by switching to a different provider offering a lower interest rate. Similar savings are there to be made if you make additional capital repayments. Remember: most of your monthly mortgage payment is interest and only takes a little off the capital balance. But when you make additional payments, they go straight to reducing the outstanding capital. By chipping away at the capital, thus reducing the size of the ball chained to your ankle, the interest also starts to shrink. This means that more money from each and every monthly payment goes to pay for your property and not bankers' bonuses.

The size of the sum of interest is governed by three variables: the size of the loan (more money borrowed equals more interest), the length of time the loan will be held for and the interest percentage. If one or more of those variables can be reduced, it will shrink the amount of interest.

Now that that causal relationship has been firmly established, you would be wise to start making additional repayments sooner rather than later. For the longer you leave it the more money you will have to pay in interest. And interest, remember, is a fictious variable that exerts real-world consequences: what is conjured in the mind of a financier will cost you in time and physical labour. The concluding section of this lengthy tip aims to teach you how to start making additional payments. Together we will explore a range of options that, if acted upon, could, over the life of your mortgage, save you thousands in unnecessary interest payments. Not only save you thousands but bring about the premature termination of the dreaded death pledge.

How to make additional mortgage payments

Before we take a look at the methods you can use to bring down the size of our mortgage, you need to know that when you implement one of these methods, nothing is going to happen overnight. When you resolve to make additional payments, the initial reducing effect those payments exert against on your mortgage is imperceptible. For a number of years it'll seem as though nothing is happening and you'll start to ask yourself if it wouldn't be better to spend that money on some species of consumerism. It's at moments like this, when your resolve starts packing its bags, that you ought to remind yourself that it's the patient penny-pincher who reaps the financial fruit. In ten years' time, when your mortgage is a meek shadow of its former self, you will commend yourself highly for having maintained the discipline to stay the course.

Every single penny that is spent on a thing you don't need could go to reducing the mortgage, thus moving you one step closer to freedom from what is, for the majority of people, the most tyrannical and burdensome of all financial oppressors.

Okay, we have at our disposal two options by which we can wage war.

First, you could increase your monthly payments. You could, as of this minute (as long as you are reading this on a weekday during banking hours), contact your mortgage provider and demand that they increase your monthly payments by X amount. Whatever figure X represents will automatically go to reducing your outstanding mortgage balance. If you were to raise your payments by, say, £50 a month, that would reduce your balance by £600 a year – or £3,000 in five years – or £6,000 in ten years. And don't forget: the interest will shrink commensurate with the mortgage. It's like a two-birds-one-stone situation. Reduce one, reduce both.

The drawback with increasing monthly payments arises for those who have little savings and/or don't have much money spare after paying the bills; you could be left short and deprived of your safety net. The last thing you want to do is run the risk of getting in debt or dipping into your overdraft. That would, of course, defeat this whole enterprise.

The second way to reduce your mortgage may be a better option for some: you pay an annual lump sum. You could open a separate savers account and deposit small sums into it at the end of each month, but only when it is possible for you to do so. At the end of the year, assuming that you are in a financially stable position, you could take the money in that savings account, however insignificant it is, and make a one-off capital repayment. Again, as with the additional monthly payments, any lump sum that you pay to your lender will be deducted from the remaining balance.

The one major stumbling block with the lump sum option is that it can be bloody hard to hand over your cash to the bank once you've struggled to scrimp and save it. This is what I call the Gollum Syndrome, so named in honour of that lecherous little goblin-like creature from *The Lord of the Rings* who just couldn't let go of his ring. At the end of the year, when it comes to transferring a few thousand pounds into the seemingly bottomless pit of your mortgage, you will almost certainly suffer from the Gollum Syndrome. To overcome the temptation to keep your money, a psychological war will have to be waged and overcome. Few people ever win that war.

But why do so few people win that war? Daniel Kahneman, in his book *Thinking, Fast and Slow*, talks at great length about our predisposition for certainty and our inherent inability to make favourable rational decisions. For example, when people are given the option of £80 now or, say, £120 in a week's time, the vast majority, around 90%, will take the £80. Why? Well, with all the wisdom and insight that Kahneman's book indubitably contains, the only plausible explanation is that we've evolved to take what's going while the going's good (and most people are miserable at delaying gratification) – though that £120 is enticing, it is not, unlike the £80, *guaranteed*. After all, I could get mowed down by the No. 10 bus tomorrow and when I'm lying on the road a mangled mess moaning in agony, I'll be really pissed off that I didn't take that £80 while I could.

But when making repayments remember to ascertain exactly how much you can pay back before incurring an early redemption charge (or ERC for brevity). If you've recently stepped foot on the property ladder and are not familiar with the vernacular, an ERC is a penalty that providers use to deter the dutiful borrower from paying too much off the capital. Why, you might well ask in your exploitable naïveté, why would they want to do that? After all, isn't it the aim of the provider's game to get their fictitious money back? *Yes* . . . and *No*. Let me clarify. Yes, the aim of this fixed game is for the provider to get their money back, just not too quickly. For, if the capital is cleared early, they will lose out on interest payments. By way of example, if a barrower took out, say, £200,000 over 30 years and fixed for five years at an interest rate of 3%, the bank would enjoy a fat return of somewhere in the region of £15,000 – in pure interest profit! Sickening I know. By brining the capital down too quickly the borrower would deprive the provider of their pound of flesh, and no provider will tolerate that. So, to avoid being stung by an ERC (or equivalent), firstly find out the bounds of your repayment clause.

* * *

If you were to ask me to condense my advice on mortgages into one concise sentence it is this: do not take on a mortgage that exceeds 5X your yearly income and start making additional payments, whether they're monthly or an annual lump sum, and do it now, for you will regret it in years to come if you don't. That I promise.

Tip 10: Advance Your Knowledge

Henry David Thoreau wrote, 'To read well, that is, to read true books in a true spirit, is a noble exercise, and one that will tax the reader more than any exercise which the customs of the day esteem.' And he wasn't wrong. I love those words and have made them my mantra.

We should always be striving to improve our stock of knowledge; after all, knowledge is latent power. Those who are well read, or who at least make reading a regular habit, tend to do better across all contemporary modalities of measuring socio-economic success. Warren Buffett, billionaire investor and founder of Berkshire Hathaway, one of the world's leading investment firms, purportedly read hundreds of books on investing before the age of eighteen and even now, in his eighties, he habitually reads in excess of six hours a day. Chess grandmaster Bobby Fischer was another voracious reader. By the tender age of sixteen he'd read over a thousand books on chess and beaten some of the best players in the sport. Today, over forty-seven years since he took the title of grandmaster, many consider Fischer to be the greatest chess player of all time.

Now I'm not drawing a causal link between reading and success (I read for two to three hours most days and I'm neither a billionaire nor chess grandmaster). And I'm not implying that if you metamorphose into a bookworm and gorge your way through a library you'll become rich and wonderful and have everything you ever dreamed of. Contrary to the illusion being propagated by the ever-expanding legion of 'entrepreneurs' reading will not guarantee success. Why? Because reading is a passive activity. Beyond augmenting your stock of knowledge and illuminating your understanding it is non-productive: when we read, we are consuming not producing. Hence the reason I said knowledge is *latent* power and not, as Francis Bacon erroneously maintained, power in and of itself. Let's take the example of Mr Buffett and Mr Fischer. Yes, they were both insatiable consumers of knowledge, but more importantly they were obsessive *practitioners*. Before they'd sprouted a pube or popped their first pimple they were mastering their respective professions.

Therein we discover the secret! Knowledge acquisition in itself is not enough. For knowledge stored in the brain will, over time, either evaporate or stagnate. It must be allowed to flow and, like a hydrostatic dam, be used to generate energy and action.

The advice that is most often given by financial gurus is to read and continue to learn. Don't make the mistake of thinking that you know it all and that your way is the best way. The world is changing at an unprecedented rate, and what might be sagacious advice today could well be rendered obsolete tomorrow. Thus we must continue to expand our knowledge and forcibly push back the stubborn boundaries of ignorance. And to do that, you'll be relieved to learn, doesn't require you to spend six hours a day reading. As Arnold Bennett advised a hundred years ago, swapping the daily paper (or TV programme) for a book will more than suffice to set you on the right tracks.

Okay, lecture over. Below is a list of books that I believe contain valuable and highly useful information that could make a dramatic difference in your life. And not just a financial difference either. Remember, the single most important ingredient of financial success isn't fiscal acumen or knowing how to exploit the 'system'. The single most important ingredient is personal discipline.

Letters From a Stoic (Seneca)

> Anything of which you are entitled the owner is in your possession but not your own; for there is no strength in that which is weak, nor anything lasting and invincible in that which is frail. We must lose our lives as surely as we lose our property, and this, if we understand the truth, is itself a consolation. Lose it with equanimity; for you must lose your life also.

The best teacher on cultivating discipline was Seneca, a sickly toga-clad philosopher who lived two thousand years ago. 'Adam,' I can hear the literary aficionado ask, 'why Seneca? You must justify this choice.' Well, having read his letters, some multiple times, I feel qualified to state with unflinching confidence that they contain a veritable ocean of wisdom – worldly wisdom; wisdom about life, about living; advice on how to be a better person, how to mitigate fear, how to become self-sufficient, strong, stoical, able to face the many slings and arrows that life inevitably throws at us. Truly, the writings of Seneca have had the single greatest impact on my life. How many books can we say that of?

Good Strategy/Bad Strategy (Richard Rumelt)

> Strategy is 'a way through a difficulty, an approach to overcoming an obstacle, a response to a challenge.'

It wasn't until I read this book that I realised just how important it is to develop a strategy prior to pursuing a goal or tackling a problem. Doing either without first formulating a strategy is the equivalent of groping blindly in the dark, hoping to find the car keys you've dropped. Strategy can act like a torch, better enabling you to find what you're searching for. Rumelt, one of the foremost leaders in the field of strategy, deftly guides us through the technical process of strategic development. On this interesting journey he stops to show us examples of what constitutes good strategy and bad strategy through various case studies that he was personally involved in. He also provides us with the tools to enable us to begin fashioning our very own strategies. In addition, Rumelt rectifies perhaps the single most prevalent mistake made by strategists: confounding 'strategy' with 'goal'. The easiest way to circumvent this is to view the goal as a destination – static, inert and existing somewhere beyond the horizon – and the strategy as the map and resources that can help you get there. A goal is a passive aspiration whereas strategy is active pursuit; at its essence, says Rumelt, 'strategy is about action, about doing something' (p. 87).

Rich Dad Poor Dad (Robert Kiyosaki)

> I was disturbed by how much the adults did not know about the basics of simple accounting and investing. They had difficulty grasping the relationship between their Income Statement and their Balance Sheet. As they bought and sold assets, they had trouble remembering that each transaction could impact their monthly cash flow. I thought, how many millions of people are out there in the real world struggling financially, only because they have never been taught these subjects?

Kiyosaki exploded onto the financial scene with his myth-busting wisdom that contradicted conventional financial orthodox teachings. For example, before Kiyosaki came along the gold standard in financial advice was that your house was an asset, so hurry the hell up and get on the property ladder, you dumb schmuck! I remember being told as much by a friend who worked, of all things, as a mortgage broker.

But Kiyosaki challenged the paradigm.

In fact, he turned it on its head. Thanks to his insight we can see that this advice is at best fallacious and at worst expensive. How can anything be classed as an asset if it costs you double to possess it? Assets, by definition, should confer the owner a greater return on investment.

Kiyosaki also challenged the belief that successful people are the ones who go to work and exchange their labour for a pay cheque. The problem with this approach, as he points out, is that really the only way to inflate your income is either by working more hours or blowing your boss for a pay rise. Kiyosaki erodes the foundation of this erroneous belief and suggests ways of becoming your own financial master – such as by building a portfolio of passive income streams.

> **Passive income** is **income** that requires no effort to earn and maintain.
>
> Wikipedia

I feel compelled to advance a word of warning regarding Kiyosaki's advice on investing. He makes it sound all so simple. Pop a penny in the slot, pull the lever and out gushes hundreds of pounds. Who wouldn't be enticed to take a nibble at a fat juicy worm like this: 'A few individuals are getting ridiculously rich from nothing, just ideas and agreements. If you ask many people who trade stocks or other investments for a living, they see it done all the time. Often, millions can be made instantaneously from nothing' (p. 152). Millions from nothing? Sign me up! Oh wait, I forgot. I live in a place called *reality*.

What Kiyosaki neglects to tell his readers is that those few people have probably spent many years researching the market and, more importantly, they're in the position to make millions from nothing (if that's even possible; I remain sceptical). His advice on investing in stocks is, I believe, reckless. If you think I'm being overcautious, consider what Charlie Munger, Warren Buffett's right-hand man, said of trading: 'If you take the modern world where people are trying to teach you to come in and trade actively in stocks, well, I regard that as roughly equivalent to trying to induce a bunch of young people to start off on heroin'.[6]

Principles (Ray Dalio)

> Before I begin telling you what I think, I want to establish that I'm a 'dumb shit' who doesn't know much relative to what I need to know.

Yes, Ray Dalio is the poster boy of investing and I've just spent the preceding paragraph warning anyone willing to listen of the potential perils of gambling on the stock exchange. Thus, after giving your head a good scratch, you might well ask what's with the contradiction? Though the larger portion of *Principles* is dedicated to the documentation of the author's ascension to the fiscal empyrean, which saw him climb the long ladder of trading stocks and shares, the book presents a valuable ethos, an ethos that transcends the parochial world of Wall Street. 'Principles,' Dalio tells us, 'are fundamental truths that serve as the foundation for behaviour that gets you what you want out of life.'

The guiding principles that Dalio developed to navigate the stock market could be applied to any area of life. Many of them are not remotely related to investing but serve as sound advice. For example, who wouldn't benefit from inviting into their life Principle 1.3: *Be radically open-minded and radically transparent*. In addition to offering first-class insights into investing and to

---

[6] 'Charlie Munger: Teaching young people to actively trade stocks is like starting them on heroin', *CNBC*, 14 February 2019:
https://www.cnbc.com/2019/02/14/charlie-munger-teaching-young-people-to-trade-stocks-is-like-to-starting-them-on-heroin.html. Last accessed: 30 November 2020.

sharing his principles, Dalio also gives us a lesson on economics. He does a brilliant job at making the complicated accessible.

Think and Grow Rich (Napoleon Hill)

> Failure comes to those who indifferently allow themselves to become failure conscious.

Napoleon Hill's epic *Think and Grow Rich* is widely regarded as the primum mobile of success books. One could very well argue that it catalysed the genre and is responsible for that great edifice of success and self-help literature that looms large in almost every bookstore. *Think and Grow Rich* is, at its heart, a treatise on self-empowerment – that is, taking charge of your life and becoming the master of your own fate. 'Those who pick themselves up after defeat and keep on trying, arrive – and the world cries, "Bravo! I knew you could do it!".' Hill drops many lines like this throughout the three hundred-odd pages of the book. It's as if he is subtly trying to rewire your subconscious with self-belief. But then this would not be a surprise, for Hill believed that 'autosuggestion', the action of repeatedly reaffirming one's intrinsic worth, 'is the agency of control through which an individual may voluntarily feed his of her subconscious mind on thoughts of a creative nature, or, by neglect, permit thoughts of a destructive nature to find their way into the garden of the mind.' Yes, the book does transcend the realms of reality in places, but it's worth a read nonetheless.

> When defeat comes, accept it as a signal that your plans are not sound, rebuild those plans, and set sail once more toward your coveted goal.
>
> Napoleon Hill

* * *

I hope these reading suggestions will be of use to you. My intention here has been to provide the knowledge traveller with some ideas of new topics to explore. And what better way to conclude one book than by feeling inspired to pick up another, to continue the journey – wherever it may lead.

About Adam James

....

Adam James has never created a company, social enterprise or even whipped-up a soufflé. He has yet to write a *#1 New York Times* bestseller – and most probably never will. He isn't a billionaire entrepreneur; hell, to his eternal shame, he's not even a millionaire, not even a hundred-thousandaire!

Adam hasn't advised government, NASA or a multinational. In short, he boasts precisely no lofty success or worldly renown. His single claim to fame was when he featured in a local paper for being one of the youngest recruits in history to complete the gruelling Royal Marines Commando basic training course, considered the longest and hardest military training in the world.

Despite his woeful list of personal achievements and character flaws, and he has many (by god *so!* many), he possesses great will and determination. Furthermore, he's a relentless trier and his ambitions are to be a good child of the earth and contribute a little something that might help someone somewhere.

When he's not working, writing and worrying over the coming environmental apocalypse and trying to convince people to transition to a plant-based diet, Adam devotes much of his spare time to a diverse range of pursuits; these include playing the guitar, exercising excessively, cycling and parsing anachronistic philosophical texts (always in the company of a cup of super strong coffee and the sweet sonorous sounds of Stevie Ray Vaughan).

References

....

Aristotle. (1980). *Nicomachean Ethics*. Oxford: Oxford World's Classics.

Bell, Daniel. (1996). *The Cultural Contradictions of Capitalism*. New York: Basic Books.

Boyle, Matthew. (2020). 'Savings statistics: Average savings in the UK 2020'. 13 August. *Finder* website. https://www.finder.com/uk/saving-statistics. Last accessed: 9 November 2020.

Buffett, Warren. (1999). 'How to Stay Out of Debt – Financial Future of American Youth'. *YouTube*. https://www.youtube.com/watch?v=IvveZr0D_9Y. Last accessed: 10 November 2020.

Dalio, Ray. (2017). *Principles*. New York: Simon & Schuster.

Franck, Thomas. (2019). 'Charlie Munger: Teaching young people to actively trade stocks is like starting them on heroin'. *CNBC*, 14 February: https://www.cnbc.com/2019/02/14/charlie-munger-teaching-young-people-to-trade-stocks-is-like-to-starting-them-on-heroin.html. Last accessed: 30 November 2020.

Fromm, Erich. (1976). *To Have or To Be*. London: Continuum.

_____. (1999). *The Art of Being*. London: Constable.

Gilovich, T. and Ross, L. (2016). *The Wisest One in the Room*. Great Britain: Oneworld.

Hill, Napoleon. (1937). *Think and Grow Rich*. New York: Ralston Books.

Holiday, Ryan and Hanselman, Stephen. (2016) *The Daily Stoic*. London: Profile Books.

Kahneman, Daniel. (2011). *Thinking, Fast and Slow*. New York: Farrar, Straus and Giroux.

Keynes, John Maynard. (2015). *The Essential Keynes*. London: Penguin Books.

Kiyosaki, Robert. (1998). *Rich Dad Poor Dad*. New York: Warner Business Books.

Marx, Karl. (1844). 'Money', in *Economic and Philosophical Manuscripts*. Marx Engels Archive. https://www.marxists.org/archive/marx/works/1844/epm/3rd.htm. Last accessed: 1 December 2020.

Mason, Paul. (2015). *PostCapitalism*. London: Penguin Books.

O'Neil, William J. (2009). *How to Make Money in Stocks*. New York & London: McGraw-Hill.

Robbins, Tony. (2016). *Money: Master the Game*. New York: Simon & Schuster.

Rumelt, Richard. (2017). *Good Strategy/Bad Strategy*. London: Profile Books.

Seneca. (2016). *Letters from a Stoic*. New York: Dover Thrift.

Tharp, Van K. (2007). *Trade Your Way to Financial Freedom*. New York: McGraw Hill.

Treanor, Jill. (2017). 'UK's £200bn consumer debt unsustainable, S&P warns'. 24 October. https://www.theguardian.com/business/2017/oct/24/uks-200bn-consumer-debt-unsustainable-sp-warns. Last accessed: 1 December 2020.

Watchdog blog. (2020). 'Bank Fraud: Easy to be a victim – hard to get your money back?'. *BBC*, 8 April: https://www.bbc.co.uk/programmes/articles/1KD40dVs0

FmtnRv4ByszLr8/bank-fraud-easy-to-be-a-victim-hard-to-get-your-money-back. Last accessed: 17 November 2020.

WRAP website. 'Reports – food waste from all sectors'. *WRAP* (Waste and Resources Action Programme). www.wrap.org.uk/content/all-sectors. Last accessed: 6 November 2020.

Index

Please note, numbers highlighted in bold correspond to charts, diagrams and/or images.

A

accounting documentation, **132**
account statement, **102–103**
accounts, review, 96–105, 132, 167
   accounts, organising, 169
   accounts, switching, 166
addiction, 150, 152
   addiction, saving, 134
affiliate marketing, 189
Ali Express, 185
Amazon, 32, 139, 182, 184, 188
archetype, financial, 113–120
Aristotle, 46, 105–106
austerity, 29–33, 43, 45

B

Bacon, Francis, 213
Bank of England, 28, 197, 198
banking, online, 133
Banksy, 116
Benedictine monk, 27
Bennett, Arnold, 95, 214
bills, 13, 16, 82, 143, 149, 158, 160
   bills, household, 99
books, monetising, 181
Buddhist, monk, 149
budget, budgeting, 64–68, 73, 86, 101, 149
   budgetary restrictions, 157, 159
Buffet, Warren, 6, 69, 147, 213, 217
buying in bulk, 145

C

Cade, Jack, (from Shakespeare's *Henry VI*), 123
capital balance, 208
   capital repayment, 210

226

capitalists, 58, 63, 114, 115, 124, 156, 186
carbon footprint, reducing, 35
car-sharing, 144
Cash, Johnny, 201
Chang, Ha-Joon (economist), 37
civil disobedience, 156
common sense, 11
conspicuous consumerism, 110, 173
consumerism, 108, 153, 156, 186
   consumerism, unnecessary, 149
   consumer, 114, 122
   consumer, orgasm, 134
   consuming, knowledge, 213
credit cards, 16, 29, 60, 69–74, 132, 149
credit consolidation, 74–80
cycling (the benefits), 38, 39

D

Dalio, Ray, 6, 10, 218
debt, 1, 3, 13, 14, 16, 22, 24, 36, 57, 70, 80–81, 97, 128, 147, 173
   household debt, 1
   personal debt, 33, 52, 75, 120
Diagnostic & Statistical Manual of Mental Health (DSM), 31
Dickens, Charles, 15, 109

direct debits, 134, 137, 159–160, 164, 167, 171
   direct debit allocation, 170
   direct debit allocation flow chart, **170**
discipline, 14, 16, 20, 53, 58, 68, 71, 167
   discipline, monetary, 75, 87, 88
   self-discipline, 12, 99, 107, 108, 146, 151, 154, 157
Dionysus, 107
drop-shipping, 184–185
Drucker, Peter, F., 129, 139

E

early redemption charge, 211
eBay, 139, 184
ecommerce, 183, 185
Einstein, Albert, 85
employment, 20, 21
energy conservation, 142
entrepreneur, 181
environment, 144
Epictetus, 26
epicurean, 11
equity release, 196
equity, negative, 202

F

Facebook, 184
fasting (abstentions), 149
Feynman, Richard, P., 146

Fiennes, Ranulph, 'greatest living explorer', 94
financial crash (2008), 7, 33, 58, 198, 207
financial fasting, 16
financial health, 155
financial literacy, 97
financial mismanagement, 25
financial planning, 168
financial self-management, 12
financial strategy, 1, 16, 18, 23
financial wastage, 156
first time buyer, 206
Fischer, Bobby, 213
food waste, 41
fraud, 100
   fraud, detecting, 132
   fraudulent activity, 101
Fromm, Erich, 122–123

G

Gilovich, Thomas, 174
Gödel, Kurt, 145
Goldilocks, 86, 88
Gollum (syndrome), 210–211
Google, 191
Gould, Stephen, Jay, 184
Gray, Albert, E. N., 89
Greek philosophers, 26, 105
Guns and Roses, 138
gym membership, 163

H

habits, 89–96, 139, 142

habits, good/bad diagram, **90**
habits, spending, 151, 154
Henry, Jules, 58
Hill, Napoleon, 219–202
hobby (how to monetise), 179
Hood, Robin, 183

I

Ibsen, Henrik, 109
idiocy, financial, **116, 118**
interest rate, 71, 73, 83, 192, 193, 197
investment, 200, 201, 203
   investment portfolio, 7, 8

J

Johnson, Dr Samuel, 74
Jones, Paul Tudor, 6
Joneses (keeping up with), 151, 171

K

Kahneman, Daniel, 211
Keynes, John Maynard, 3, 6
King, Mervin, 98
Kiyosaki, Robert, 97–98, 216
knowledge, improving, 213

L

Laissez-faire, 14, 97
Lake Garda, 143
laptop lifestyle, 189

loan weight value calculation, 76–78
London School of Economics, 4

M

Marx, Karl, 115, 125–126
marathon, 130
marketing, campaign, 22
minimalism, 43
see also 'simple living', 108–109
money, 23, 30, 36, 85, 125, 147
money management, 51, 141
money, spending, 61, 141
money, wastage, 163
mortgage, 29, 83, 84, 190–212
mortgage, additional payments, 209
mortgage broker, 193, 216
mortgage, capital repayment, 195–196
mortgage, buy-to-let, 200–201
mortgage, fixed interest rate, 197
mortgage, interest-only, 199
mortgage, shared equity/partnership, 204–205
mortgage, variable interest rate, 197
motivation, 20, 75, 129, 152
Mount Everest, 94

Munger, Charlie, 217

N

Netflix, 25, 27, 32

O

O'Neil, William, 10, 205
online, 189
overdraft, 23, 25, 29, 33, 36, 97, 120, 130, 149

P

Packard, Vance, 186
parents, teaching financial literacy, 98
Pareto 80/20 law, 6
passive income, 217
Pavlov, Ivan, 188
Plato, 105
physical fitness, 163, 165
pollution, 111
positive reinforcement, 96
procrastination, 86
productivity, 152, 213
prohibition, 156
Protestant ethic, 80

Q

R

Robbins, Tony, 10
Ross, Lee, 174

Royal Marines Commandos, 120, 148
Rumelt, Richard, 18, 92, 215–216

S
Sass, Louis, 110
S&P 500, 6
savings, 13, 21, 28, 30, 52–55, 83, 88, 134, 210
   savings account flow chart, **55**
   saving, in the household, 34–37
secondary income, 203
self-help, 178
self-sufficiency, 175
Seneca, 43, 45, 107, 158, 175, 214, 215
Sisyphus, 88
social media, 172, 184
Socrates, 105
spending fast, 149
   spending fast duration guidelines **154**
Stern, Laurence, 190
stock market, 6, 9
strategy, 215
Stoicism, 26, 43, 107
sub-prime mortgage catastrophe, 207
supplementary income, 201
sweatshop, 124

T
Tharp, Van. K., 10, 109, 113
The Economist, 8
Thoreau, David, Henry, 137, 212
triathlon, 180

U

V
Vaughan, Stevie Ray, 115
Vianney, St. Jean-Baptiste-Marie, 46
vices, 121
VISIBILITY Board, **161**

W
Wall Street, 218
Wild, Oscar, 105, 111
World Wide Web, 11

X

Y
YouTube, 178, 181, 189

Z
zeitgeist, prevailing, 110

Printed in Great Britain
by Amazon